ROUTLEDGE LIBRARY EDITIONS:
AGING

I0127786

Volume 30

ACTIVITY, HEALTH
AND FITNESS
IN OLD AGE

ACTIVITY, HEALTH AND FITNESS IN OLD AGE

JEAN A. MACHEATH

Routledge
Taylor & Francis Group
LONDON AND NEW YORK

First published in 1984 by Croom Helm Ltd

This edition first published in 2024
by Routledge
4 Park Square, Milton Park, Abingdon, Oxon OX14 4RN

and by Routledge
605 Third Avenue, New York, NY 10158

Routledge is an imprint of the Taylor & Francis Group, an informa business

British Library Cataloguing in Publication Data
A catalogue record for this book is available from the British Library

ISBN: 978-1-032-67433-9 (Set)
ISBN: 978-1-032-72922-0 (Volume 30) (hbk)
ISBN: 978-1-032-72926-8 (Volume 30) (pbk)
ISBN: 978-1-003-42307-2 (Volume 30) (ebk)

DOI: 10.4324/9781003423072

Publisher's Note
The publisher has gone to great lengths to ensure the quality of this reprint but points out that some imperfections in the original copies may be apparent.

Disclaimer
The publisher has made every effort to trace copyright holders and would welcome correspondence from those they have been unable to trace.

Activity, Health and Fitness in Old Age

JEAN A. MACHEATH

CROOM HELM
London & Canberra
ST. MARTIN'S PRESS
New York

© 1984 Jean A. Macheath
Croom Helm Ltd, Provident House, Burrell Row,
Beckenham, Kent BR3 1AT
Croom Helm Australia, PO Box 391, Manuka,
ACT 2603, Australia

British Library Cataloguing in Publication Data

Macheath, Jean A.
   Activity, health and fitness in old age.
   1. Aged – Care and hygiene
   I. Title
   613'.0438   RA777.6
   ISBN 0-7099-1783-X

Library of Congress Cataloging in Publication Data

Macheath, Jean A.
   Activity, health, and fitness in old age.

   Bibliography: p.
   Includes index.
   1. Aged--Care and hygiene. 2. Physical fitness for
the aged. 3. Exercise for the aged. 4. Aged--Attitudes.
5. Aged--Care and hygiene--England. 6. Physical fitness
for the aged--England. 7. Exercise for the aged--England.
8. Aged--England--Attitudes. I. Title.
RA564.8.M32 1984   613'.0438   83-40128
ISBN 0-312-00390-0

Printed and bound in Great Britain

CONTENTS

FIGURES AND TABLES

Figures

Tables

FOREWORD

Jean Macheath has done an unusual thing. Instead of
relying on sterotypes of old age, she has taken the
trouble to ask old people themselves about their
activities and attitudes to exercise and fitness in
old age. Their positive responses were in marked
contrast to the negative expectations of middle-aged
staff who come in contact with old people. This
contrast present a potential hazard in setting
realistic goals for rehabilitation for the elderly
and this pioneer study is a helpful step towards
remedying this problem.

I am very happy to commend this book to Health,
Education and Social Services staff who help to
support the increasing numbers of old people in
today's society.

Marion Hildick Smith M.D. F.R.C.P.
Consultant Physician in Geriatric Medicine
Nunnery Fields Hospital, Canterbury, Kent.

TO

SARAH, LUCY

and GERTRUDE

PREFACE

In order for the elderly to live independent lives in the community and enjoy their freedom they must be able to perform a variety of physical tasks. The maintenance of these basic physical activities is the ultimate responsibility for every member of society, for neglect will affect their quality of life as they personally adapt to the ageing process.[1] However, not all individuals age at the same rate, nor do they lose functions in the same order or at the same time of life.
The D.H.S.S. (1978) suggests that:

an important objective of the Health and personal Social Services is to enable people to maintain independent lives in the community for as long as possible.

All the Health, Education and Social Services staff having contact with the elderly should be offering them positive advice regarding the important role of physical activity in the maintenance of their independence and freedom in the community. Only if every member of the team is encouraging the elderly to maintain their activity levels in a positive way will an active approach to treatment and rehabilitation be promoted. This will only be possible if the staff concerned have the relevant knowledge and understanding of the elderly, their lifestyles, their beliefs, and their attitudes.
This volume encompasses the findings of a descriptive study undertaken in one District Health Authority in South East England of many aspects of activity in relation to ageing. The activities engaged in by the elderly and the staff who work with them, together with the beliefs of these two

populations regarding activities of the elderly, are analysed, compared and discussed. These are followed by comparisons of the views of health, good physical condition and the effects of exercise on health of the elderly and the staff who work with them in a variety of situations.

The text has a dual thesis. First, just as an individual's interests change in the thirty years from 25 to 55 years of age, so will they probably change just as much in the following thirty years, or from 65 to 95 years of age. This text highlights that the "elderly" cannot, or should not, all be considered under this one umbrella term when the many different physical activities are to be planned or discussed. Secondly, in order to be in a position to offer positive advice to their elderly patients /clients those staff in the Health, Education and Social Services must appreciate that the elderly often have totally different interests, attitudes, and beliefs regarding activity from themselves. This text compares and contrasts such differences with a view to assisting such staff to come to terms with them, understanding them, and thus be better equipped to talk to their patients/clients in terms that are more readily comprehended and accepted.

Such a text is primarly for those in the caring professions, but it is also anticipated that those in allied professions in the Health, Education, and Social Services involved in the rehabilitation and support of the elderly in a variety of ways would also find the contents useful and thought provoking. It is in no way exhaustive, but it was felt that it would (1) answer some of the pertinent questions of immediate relevance to the training of those staff who advise the elderly regarding mobility and fitness to enable them to live independent lives in the community, (2) highlight some of the areas of concern and (3) indicate that a great deal of further research is urgently required in the many aspects of not only the current generations of elderly but also future generations of elderly.

These pertinent questions include:-
(a) Which activities are participated in by the elderly and the staff who work with them?
(b) How often are these activities pursued?
(c) What are the beliefs of health and good physical condition?
(d) What are the attitudes to exercise?
(e) How are these beliefs and attitudes related to particular groups of staff?
(f) How does age affect participation in different

forms of physical activity?

With the current team approach to care of the elderly, it is important that all staff appreciate the many different understandings of elderly participation in activities of their peers in other relevant professions, in order that they can all work to the same end - i.e. rehabilitating the elderly in order that they can enjoy their independence in their own community throughout old age.

The general plan of the text leads one from the definitions of health and fitness over the past two decades to the discussion of activity patterns of the elderly in that same time span as illustrated through research and reports. This forms a sound platform from which to consider current activity patterns, attitudes to exercise and definitions of health and fitness, as reflected in an investigation in one District Health Authority and current research reports. The ramifications for the future rehabilitation of elderly individuals and service provision are explored. In referring to an elderly person, 'she' has been used in preference to 'he', simply because there are more female elderly.

If it provokes a thought, stirs a conscience, or encourages change, however small, it will have been well worthwhile.

ACKNOWLEDGEMENTS

Such an undertaking is not possible without the
support, encouragement, advice, and assistance of
many individuals and groups over a considerable
period of time. I am most grateful to each and every
one of them for all the time they have so willingly
given me.

The research was made possible through a grant
from the Health Education Council (No: 792).

I am indebted to the many members of the
Canterbury and Thanet District Health Authority who
assisted me and offered advice throughout the study
namely: Dr. M. Hildick Smith and Dr. J. Pritchard
(Consultant Geriatricians); Mrs. M. Ramsey and Mr. J.
Hodsen (Senior Nursing Officers); and Mr. N. Murless
(Administrator). Without their support and guidance
the subsequent investigation and presentation would
not have been possible. My thanks are due, too, to
the many staff and elderly with whom I have worked in
the Geriatric Units and Clubs within the District
Health Authority over the past four years. My task
was certainly made easier and pleasant through the
co-operation and friendliness of all the staff and
elderly in the different situations. They were
welcoming, very willing, interested and patient
participants who were truly marvellous to work with.

Processing data is a time consuming and
specialist activity. This could not have been
achieved without the valuable advice, encouragement
and guidance given by Mrs. A. Hawkins of the
Department of Statistics and Computing at the
University of London Institute of Education.

Mr. Alan Beattie of the University of London
gave unstintingly of his time to offer guidance and
advice in the preparation and planning stages;
scholarly criticism throughout the collation and
presentation stages of the material; and support,

encouragement, from start to finish. Without such support, guidance and assistance it would have been very difficult indeed. The results discussed in Chapter 9 involved responses to open ended questions. To assist with the independent classification of these responses three Physical Educationalists under Mrs. C. Alloway gave readily of their time. I am very grateful for the time and effort given by these individuals in the pursuit of a soundly based classification for this aspect of the material. Reading and commenting constructively on such a script is no easy task. I am indebted to Mr. J. Wright, Principal Lecturer in Movement Studies at Nonington College for giving so readily of his time to undertake this onerous task in a most pleasant and helpful manner.

At each and every stage I have been most fortunate to enjoy the fullest co-operation with all whom I have been privileged to work. It is gratifying to know that one can approach so many individuals over a long period of time and have such positive responses to my requests for assistance. Without such assistance and co-operation the research undertaken and the resulting script would certainly not have reached fruition.

Jean A Macheath

Chapter One

PATTERNS OF ACTIVITY PARTICIPATION: AN INTRODUCTION

> We have aimed to keep old people active and
> independent in their own houses ... Everyone in
> our society, whether young or old, is both
> active and dependent, and the proportions in
> which activity and dependence are combined are a
> matter of degree and individual circumstances.
> (D.H.S.S. 1978)

In order for the elderly to live individual and
independent lives in their community, they must be
able to perform a variety of physical activities. The
maintenance of these basic physical activities is the
ultimate responsibility of every member of society
for neglect of them for any length of time will
affect the very quality of life as they personally
adapt to the ageing process. However, this adaptation
will be at differing rates for each individual for
she will lose functions in differing orders and at
differing rates to her peers.

Doctors, nurses, health visitors, and their
aides, together with dentists, chiropodists,
opticians, physiotherapists and their assistants,
along with all the other such professionals, are all
involved in the provision of the necessary health
services to improve and/or maintain the quality of
life for each individual as long as possible into and
throughout old age. Social Services are provided by
an equally diverse group of people including social
workers, home helps, meals on wheels staff, and
Social Security office staff. All these Health and
Social Services staff together with the staff in the
Education Services providing classes for the elderly
could be, and indeed should be involved in offering
positive advice and encouragement to their elderly
clients particularly regarding the important role of
the many physical activities of daily living and

1

recreation in the maintenance of their independence and freedom in their community. Only if everyone is encouraging the elderly to maintain their activity levels in a positive manner will "an active approach to treatment and rehabilitation" (D.H.S.S. 1978) be promoted.

On retirement one is often wished well for a long and happy retirement coupled with the advice to enjoy a well earned rest. This attitude by one's peers discourages the retired individual from considering participation in many forms of excellent physical activity. It is assumed that all retired people will be less active than their working peers! Gore (1978) suggests that these social expectations are misguided whilst Shephard (1978) believes the perceptions regarding levels of activity of the elderly themselves are also related to these cultural expectations. Throughout life the young and the middle aged participation in physical activity is very much accepted today but, in marked contrast, social attitudes and fear regarding physical activity throughout retirement militate against participation.

Hearnshaw (1972) indicates that lack of physical activity in old age is a more serious disadvantage than social restrictions. Movement aids the maintenance and/or rehabilitation of general health (Gore 1977). Bassey (1978) supports the view that there is a strong correlation between activity levels and physical condition throughout old age. The body of each individual was built for activity right throughout life and indeed requires activity to ensure its proper functioning. The World Health Organization (1978) suggests that physical activity is a positive health criterion whilst the lack of such activity is considered to be a health risk factor.

"To take it easy" on retirement might well be interpreted then as "to take health risks" indicating a need to educate society of the consequences of giving such advice to their peers and seniors as they retire from the work force. It is of vital importance that those staff in the Health and Social Services working with the elderly throughout their old age understand the relevance of such advice.

"Old Age" is a term that covers a vast range of people. It generally includes anyone over statutory retirement age (i.e.: sixty years of age for women and sixty five years of age for men). Some of the very old people are still very active both physically and mentally. However, others well below sixty years of age are in poor health, suffering from forgetfulness, lacking in energy and vitality, and are often described as "dodderers", "squares", or "old fashioned". From a social point of view, those of statutory pension age form a natural group (Hazell 1960). These were the age bands used by Miller (1963), Townsend and Wedderburn (1965), and Shanas et al (1968) in their studies of the elderly. The World Health Organization (1974) divided this vast range of men and women into two groups:

Elderly, aged 60 years to 74 years
Aged, aged over 75 years.

This or similar divisions may solve the problems posed by the ever increasing numbers of men and women living well into retirement and on into old age, for the needs of the sixty year olds will differ widely from the needs of those in their nineties and even hundreds.

The most impressive characteristic of old age is the diversity (Richardson 1964) for there is no standardised old person either man or woman (Anjeleu 1965). The problems of such a diverse group of individuals cannot be considered in a stereotyped manner for they often vary from week to week according to their health or the time of the year (Bracey 1966). Sometimes it is necessary and important to categorise older people in various ways, but this totally ignores the basic fact that there are many ways of growing old.

Shanas et al (1968) remind one that old age and illness are in no way synonymous. Shephard (1978) suggests that many cultures decree that habitual activity will diminish with ageing. This view is supported by Zaborowski et al (1962) who also indicate that leisure activities change with cultural expectations. In general terms the elderly do not function as well as the young or middle aged. Shanas et al (1968) indicate that old age though is not necessarily a period of marked decline physically for everyone. Some elderly can, and do, perform equally as well as younger men and women into and throughout old age. The World Health Organization (1978) suggests that the decline in physical activity with age is more marked in leisure time pursuits than in the activities of daily living, and that while the types of activity change little with increasing age, the time spent on physical recreation is less and the elderly are less energetic when actually participating. The only exceptions given were walking and gardening.

The many different organisations and their

3

individual staff members involved with the provision of care and a satisfactory quality of life for each elderly individual in her own community must have the same positive approach to, and understanding of, physical activity into and throughout old age. Each individual elderly person will have a different perception of what this "quality of life" means for her in relation to her own attitudes to that life and the immediate environment in which she lives. Staff must take cognizance of these attitudes and perceptions of the elderly individuals for rehabilitation or maintenance of the status quo to be successful.

In offering advice to the elderly, Health Services staff must

provide the client with genuine understanding without the use of indoctrination attempts or emotional manipulation; it must leave the client with total awareness of the range of behavioural options open to him/her without attempting to bias the client's choice.

(Tones 1977)

Hochbaum (1971) suggests that such advice will be effective if the majority of the elderly were influenced by it and thus making positive decisions to modify their behaviour. In relation to physical activities, the advice would prove effective if the majority of elderly people maintained their levels of activity throughout old age and enjoyed fully their independence and freedom in the community.

If those staff in the Health, Education and Social Services appreciate the need for behavioural modification, they will be better placed to attempt to encourage the elderly to continue to participate in the physical activities of daily living and recreation into and throughout old age. However, behavioural modification of the staff concerned is dependent on their being able to receive advice and assistance through basic and post basic and In Service courses.

There appears to be very little known, or reported, about the types of activity the current generation of elderly people are actually involved in throughout old age, nor the types of activity they feel they could, and should, be participating in. Similarly, little appears to be known about how the elderly themselves see their own health or how participating in physical activities affects their health. Baumann (1961) compared a small group of

4

elderly individuals and a group of medical students in the United States whilst Macheath (1978) considered the concepts of fitness held by a select group of elderly people in South East England.

The beliefs and attitudes of the staff who work with the elderly in a variety of situations and the elderly themselves regarding the place of physical activity and fitness throughout old age will have a considerable bearing on the future participation of many elderly individuals in rehabilitative, recreational, or daily living physical pursuits. The beliefs and attitudes of the staff will reflect both the social mores of the day and those established during their basic or post basic training. The elderly require positive advice that is meaningful and relevant to them in their individual situations if it is to be acted upon (Fletcher 1972). Attitudes and beliefs are formulated both by individuals and society generally today. How they are perceived by the elderly today is reflected in the activities they will pursue.

If advice to the elderly is to be positive and encouraging from the staff working with them, it is important that some of the key issues are understood and come to terms with. These issues include:-

(a) The differences in activity patterns between different age groups within society.

(b) The different understandings and beliefs regarding activities of the elderly held by different age groups within society.

(c) The differing concepts of health and attitudes to exercise held by the elderly and the staff who work with them.

As individuals of all ages in the Health, Education, and Social Services will be working with the widely grouped "elderly", it is of paramount importance that such issues are considered within small age bands and the many professions involved. The "elderly" need to be considered in similarly small age bands if their relevant needs are to be addressed. In the ensuing chapters consideration will be given to these key issues in order that similarities and differences may be highlighted in order that understanding may be increased and problems come to terms with.

The attitudes and beliefs of the elderly today have been developed against a background of abject poverty, hard work, danger, and wretched housing (Abrams 1978). Abrams goes on to remind one that the 30.0% who have survived to the age of seventy five years today are exceptional and atypical.

Bosanquet (1978) suggests that the aspirations of the elderly are modest but these have been contrived by society to add to a decline in health and opportunity. The attitudes of the elderly to the situations in which they find themselves stems initially from their attitude to retirement and the changed circumstances that follow retirement. These attitudes are also related to their self perception and will reflect in their attitudes to health and lifestyle, including their approach to the many physical activities involved in their daily round. Lack of activity by the elderly can be the result of many different reasons - illness, injury, disability, or just plain idleness. Whatever the reason, research has shown that the effects can have serious consequences for everyone, and especially the elderly.

The phenomena of senescence - decrease in muscle mass, reduced oxygen intake, reduced heat production, fall in total blood volume - are accelerated by senile inactivity and a lack of sufficient physical activity (Mateeg 1961). Leonardo de Vinci attributed premature ageing to lack of physical activity. Raab (1961) shows that habitual lack of physical activity leads to deficiency in the vagal cholinergic sympathetico - inhibitory mechanism which leaves the heart muscle vulnerable to injury from emotional stress; and is a major factor in coronary heart disease. Creeping obesity, a particular problem for the elderly is also attributed to a lack of physical activity.

Sufferers from degenerative joint disease who are active, appear to complain less than more sedentary sufferers (Williams and Speryn 1976). Regular activity by the elderly will alleviate joint stiffness and reduce degenerative disease (Larson and Michaelman 1973) and thus increase mobility for these individuals.

If physical activity is not part of the daily life of the elderly, then muscle atrophy (loss of functional use) occurs through disuse with serious reprocussions regarding mobility (Larson and Michaelman 1973). The latter authors also suggest that physical activity is important in the reduction of tension, stress, and fatigue all of which can result in decreased mobility. Ataxia (inability to co-ordinate body movements) is another major factor affecting mobility that can tbe the result of inactivity. Exercise can assist in increasing joint flexibility and thus mobility (Smith 1968).

Lack of mobility often leads to problems of need

in relation to daily living activities as suggested by Isaacs and Neville (1976), which are themselves excellent forms of physical activity and to be encouraged in order that independence can be maintained (Berrington Jones 1975). Many staff in the caring professions are indeed encouraging elderly to dress themselves, even if this does take rather a long time, as a means of regaining flexibility and mobility.

Activity is important in keeping muscles strong and joints mobile (Hooker 1976); relatively efficient sound postieral habits and good alignment (Smith 1968); and the prevention of osteoarthritis and athercosclerosis (Anderson 1976). The role of physical activity is becoming increasingly important as the diseases of the elderly are moving from infection to degeneration. There is growing evidence to show that the physiological benefits of increased work capacity helps to prolong the satisfactory life of the elderly (Allman and Watt 1975).

With the increasing numbers of elderly in the population each year, it can be seen that the more senescence can be retarded, the less demands this expanding population will make on the health and social services. The more the elderly can be maintained in the community with their independence, the greater will be their interest in life and the role they can play in the building of their own future. The elderly can only do this if they are mobile and able to perform the activities of daily living for themselves. Research has shown that physical activities are crucial in ensuring that the elderly are strong enough and flexible enough to cope with these activities. However, little research has been undertaken into how to achieve this state by getting across to the elderly the importance of physical activity to their continued participation in community life. The elderly of today have not had the benefits of current research in their earlier years, but they can be assisted to improve the quality of their lives through tertiary health prevention programmes.

Chapter Two

BELIEFS AND ATTITUDES REGARDING ACTIVITY AND FITNESS

> It is the members of society who must say what
> they mean by health (there are no health
> specialists) and must make the ethical and
> political choices involved.
>
> (Wilson 1975)

These members of society in saying what they mean by
health will also be indicating what they believe
affects the health of their peers in that society.
Physical activity and fitness will number among the
factors that come under consideration. Fitness
usually relates to a particular task or activity
whereas health relates to a state of being or an
ideal.

Attitudes and beliefs regarding activity and
fitness have changed and evolved over the past two
decades to include the purely medical/organic model,
the medical/biological model, the biological/dynamic
model, and the dynamic/whole person model. These
changes have been accompanied in the same time span
by changes in the many sociocultural aspects of life,
all of which have a bearing on the elderly and the
Health and Social Services provided for them. The
beliefs and attitudes held in relation to physical
activity and fitness by individuals in society will
reflect the changes in that society and the mores of
it. These will, thus, affect the advice (and its
method of presentation) given by individuals to their
patients and peers.

OLD AGE AND ILLNESS ARE NOT SYNONYMOUS

In most western cultures, old age is associated with
illness. The elderly individual is regarded as sick.
But, Shanas et al (1968) clearly indicates that old

8

age and illness are not synonymous. Old age is a period of marked physcial decline for some individuals but by no means everyone. In general terms, though, the elderly do not appear to be as well as the young or the middle aged. (Shanas et al, 1968).

On retirement one is often wished well for a long and happy retirement coupled with the advice to "take it easy" or "to enjoy a well earned rest". It is assumed that on a given day one will suddenly become less active, older, and not be able to pursue the delights of yesterday. Gore (1978) suggests that these social expectations are misguided whilst Shepard (1978) believes the perception of the elderly regarding participation in physical activities is also related to these cultural expectations.

Old age is a term that covers a vast range of individuals, for it is generally used to include anyone, male or female, above the statutory retirement age (i.e. sixty years of age for a woman and sixy five years of age for a man). Thus, encompassed in such a term are those of sixty years of age, octogenarians, nonogenarians, and even centenarians. Some very old people are still very active both mentally and physically whilst others well under sixty years of age are in poor health, suffering from forgetfulness, lacking in energy and initiative, and are often referred to by society members as "dodderers", "squares", or "old fashioned".

The most impressive characteristic of old age is its diversity (Richardson 1964) for there is no standardised old person, man or woman (Anjeleu 1965). The problems and needs of this extremely diverse collection of individuals often vary considerably not only from week to week but also according to the time of the year according to their health (Bracey 1966).

With so many differing people making up this group defined as elderly each living in their own environment, with their own accommodation to their declining physical prowess, making their own adaptations to accommodate such changes as become necessary throughout old age in order to maintain their mobility and independence in that environment (Miller (1963) suggests that this is the most prized quality in old age) illness and old age cannot be termed synonymous.

FUNCTIONING IN THE COMMUNITY RELATED TO THE PERCEPTION OF HEALTH

Functioning in the community is related to the individual's perception of health and not to her actual health state (Rose and Peterson 1965). However, there appears to be no estimate of the health of the elderly based upon function (Shanas et al 1968). There is a tendancy to treat all old people according to what they look like rather than what they feel like (Younghusband 1977). The World Health Organization (1974) says:

> The health of the elderly is best measured in terms of function - the degree of fitness rather than the extent of pathology may be used as a measure of the amount of services the aged will require from the community.

This suggests a more positive approach to health throughout old age relating it directly to the elderly in their own community setting and assuming that functioning will be possible despite pathological deterioration. Shanas et al (1968) suggest that subjective feelings are often much better indicators of the elderly individual's ability to function rather than the presence or absence of particular conditions. Such an indicator may be in terms of the elderly themselves making the judgements or those working with and observing them or both. The final judgement of the ability to function in the community in relation to the health of the elderly individual may well vary according to who is making that final judgement, their background knowledge, beliefs and attitudes.
The functioning of the elderly in their particular community is often related not to their actual health but to the elderly's perception of their own health (Rose and Peterson 1965) although some elderly will cling to "wellness" despite having serious "illness" (Shanas 1962). Thus, it appears possible to have seriously ill elderly feeling very well but looking old and ill; feeling very ill but looking spritely and well; and also looking well and feeling fine or marvellous. Each of these groups of elderly individuals would, according to Younghusband (1977) be treated differently by the community in which they function and would also function very differently in that community. Shephard (1978) suggests that the self rating of health by the elderly bears only a limited relationship to their

actual health as a result of a clinical examination. He goes to suggest too that there is a similar discrepancy between their actual and perceived exercise needs too.

ASSESSMENT OF FITNESS

Hobson and Pemberton (1955) found little difference in the self assessment of fitness in relation to blood pressure in men but there was a more marked difference in women. (Table 2.1).

A similar pattern emerges when mobility and a feeling of fitness are considered against a medical assessment of fitness as Table 2.2 illustrates.

Most elderly do not see health as an ideal state but were of the practical approach as suggested by McEwen et al (1983). Health is a social value and must be considered as such.

Many elderly individuals appear to feel fit and have unrestricted mobility and are well able to fucntion in their particular community despite being declared medically unfit as a result of a pathological condition. When clinical pathology is considered as a factor affecting function a very negative picture emerges for all age groups but especially in the over 75 years age group. Richardson (1964) found similar discrepancies between the self perception of health and restricted freedom in the community. Anderson (1955) reported that 8.7% of the elderly said they were ill whereas the doctors reported 25.2% diseased in the sample population. However, Bromley (1972) suggests that this self evaluation by the elderly of their capabilities annd health varies very much with the actual physical condition. More recent studies illustrate similar discrepancies to those already outlined. Abrams (1978) suggests that 40.0% of the elderly claim their health is good, whilst 10.0% of those aged 65-74 years and 16.0% of those aged over 75 years claim that they have no physical problem whatsoever and can, therefore, function exactly as they wish in their own communities.

The Administration on Aging (1975) suggests that fitness is many faceted and relates to:-

a quality of life; the condition that helps a person look well and feel well; to carry out his daily duties and responsibilities successfully and yet have enough physical resources to enjoy his social, cultural, and recreational interests ... and meet unusual or emergency demands.

Williams (1965) suggests that the level at which both work and recreation are pursued is related to the fitness of the individual and this has an effect on the total welfare of the community. These two approaches to defining fitness are unique to each individual and her needs in her own community environment. Earlier Bortz (1960) indicated that fitness should be defined in relation to age and normal activity.

Thus, fitness is a very personal thing which should be determined by each individual in relation to whatever activity she wishes to undertake in the community at any given time. How one perceives her fitness will, therefore, vary from one situation to another according to the activity and the situation in which it is to be undertaken. This self assessment of fitness to function at any given time in a particular environment will be subjective and variable and will undoubtedly be affected by a great many factors.

SELF ASSESSMENT OF HEALTH

Several recent studies have considered the self assessment of health rather than fitness but illustrate similar discrepancies to those outlined above. When health was related to function by the use of the Roscow Scale (Roscow and Breslau 1966) those with good functional health saw their health as good for their age. Women decline more sharply than men, but more women than men in the poorest health still saw their own health as good for their age. (Table 2.3).

According to Age Concern (1977) mean satisfaction with health changes little with age. (Table 2.4).

However, all those aged over 60 years are encompassed in one group, thus taking a very general approach to the manner in which the very diverse group of elderly individuals spanning thirty plus years assess their own satisfaction with their health. More discrete age bands in this older age group might have produced a very changed image.

HEALTH AND FITNESS

Self evaluation of health and fitness appears to vary not only from men to women but also with age and cultural background as illustrated by one of the few studies in this field by Shanas et al (1968). More British feel they are fitter for their age than their Danish or American peers and far fewer believe their health is poorer than that of their peers overseas. This may well reflect the social mores and/or beliefs and attitudes regarding health in old age highlighted in Chapter One. The Americans are more likely to report their health as poor, report less incapacity; are less willing to accept the limitations of ageing; are less content with their health; and complain about their health more than the elderly Danes or British. (Shanas et al 1968). (Table 2.5).

The mobile elderly are more likely to say their health is good but the British are twice as likely as either the Danes or the Americans to say their health is good even if they are housebound (Shanas et al 1968). With the increasing number of elderly individuals within the different ethnic groups settled in new environments overseas further comparative studies are required in order that cognizance may be taken of their different self assessments of health and fitness when related to their new environments and coupled with their background beliefs and attitudes.

PERCEPTION AND SERVICE PROVISION

It is suggested that the subjective feelings of the elderly themselves in relation to physical activity, health, and fitness are often the best indicators of how these individuals will function in the community in which they live. Little knowledge appears to be readily available in relation to these subjective feelings of the elderly, nor how they might relate to more concrete concepts of, and attitudes to, participation in activities for use as indicators to those who work with the elderly in the Health, Education and Social Services.

The changes in provision of Health and Social Services will be based upon the perceptions of the providers and administrators regarding the needs of the elderly rather than the actual perceived needs of the elderly themselves. Johnson (1976) suggests that social gerontolists are imposing values onto older people which maybe appropriate to people of work age and who bear an obligation to work, but inappropriate to those whose time is, at least in theory, all their own.

Nursing care and <u>rehabilitation</u>, together with Social Service provision, are usually based upon predetermined standards that operate nationwide regardless of the fact that elderly individuals in different parts of the country may have totally different <u>perceived health problems and needs</u>. Do the rural and urban elderly perceive their health needs to be identical? Do all elderly individuals even with the same physical disability perceive their condition as requiring the same remedy? Are the most expensive services necessarily the best for the elderly? Once social gerontologists have applied themselves to these issues, the nursing and caring professions will appreciate that:- "clients should be part of the process of diagnosing their own state, and thus having done, exercising a choice from a range of appropriate options" (Johnson 1976). The perceived needs of the elderly themselves will then be understood and resolved through the provision of appropriate Health and Social Services to the satisfaction of both the elderly individual and the caring professions.

THE CHANGING UNDERSTANDING OF FITNESS

Fitness usually relates to a particular task or activity whereas health relates to a state of being or an ideal. Wilson (1975) suggests that how health is defined has important consequences for future actions within society by both the individual and groups. For example, the methods of practice and attitudes of those Health, Education, and Social Service professions responsible for maintaining or rehabilitating the health of people of all ages will reflect their definition and understanding of health and fitness for both themselves and their clients. Concepts of physical fitness appear to have changed and evolved in the past two decades to include the purely medical/organic model, the medical/biological model, the biological/dynamic model, and the dynamic/whole person model. These changing concepts of physical fitness have been accompanied in the same period by changes in several other concepts and the sociocultural aspects of life, all of which will have a bearing on the elderly themselves as well as the health and/or social services provided for them.

The Administration on Aging (1975) suggests that fitness in old age has two facets - organic and dynamic. Organic fitness it is suggested is "good organic health, a body free from disease or infirmity, and well nourished". Dynamic fitness is described as involving "the resources to move vigorously, to do, to live energetically". Both these aspects of fitness, then, are many faceted and indicate that fitness relates to:-

> a quality of life; the condition that helps a person to look and feel well, to carry out his daily duties and responsibilities successfully and yet have enough physical resources to enjoy his social, civic, cultural, and recreational interests ... and meet unusual or emergency demands.
> (Administration on Aging, 1975)

This approach to defining fitness in 1975 appears to include many facets related to both the medical/organic and the dynamic/whole person models mentioned above. The President's Council on Fitness and Sport (1978) agrees with this multifaceted approach to defining fitness, but it also appears to have greater bias to specific aspects of the organic model along with its more general approach to the dynamic aspects of fitness, i.e.

> proper nutrition, adequate rest and relaxation, good health practices, good medical and dental care, and exercise

on the one hand and a

> measure of body's strength, stamina, and flexibility, a reflection of the ability to work with vigour and pleasure without undue fatigue, involving both mental and physical effects

on the other hand.

It is interesting to note that the President's Fitness Council (1978) definition above appears to give priority to the organic aspects over the dynamic/whole person model. This body, though, is endeavouring to persuade people of all ages, including the elderly, in the United States to take exercise as a means to a better old age when,

perhaps, the ability to do, or to work, without undue fatigue might well be more inviting.
Williams and Sperryn (1976) lean towards the dynamic/whole person aspects of the Administration on Aging (1975) definition above. They suggest that fitness is the ability to indulge in activity for as long as one felt like it without becoming distressed. Perhaps this is indicating that fitness should be a personal thing which should be determined by each individual at any given time in relation to whatever activity he/she wishes to participate in. Williams (1965) suggests that the ability to perform work has a direct bearing on an individual's ability to survive the stresses and strains imposed by the environment. He goes on to suggest that the level of activity at which both work and recreation are pursued is related to the fitness of the individual and this has resulting effects on the total welfare of his/her community. This approach clearly combines the individual, medical/organic and dynamic/whole body approach in the understanding of fitness: and can be seen as an important change to the total "individual/related to circumstances" approach of recent years.
The Health Education Council (1977) reminds us that fitness is a much misused word which can mean

anything from a vague feeling of well being as he takes a deep breath of fresh air by an open window to a sensation of comfort while taking exercise which would make an untrained man stiff for a week.

Neither Williams and Sperryn (1976) nor the Health Education Council (1977) approaches to fitness appear to consider the medical/organic model necessary to their definition, but it is inherent in the overall concept. Matthews (1973) supports this approach to fitness in suggesting it is:- "the capacity of the individual to perform given physical tasks involving muscular effort".
It would appear that the ability to perform activity without feeling distressed is central to the modern concept of physical fitness. It is clear too, that fitness is related to the individual's needs and the tasks she wishes to pursue. Thus fitness will be very different for different elderly people in different situations and also for the same elderly individual in different situations and circum-stances.
Bruner and Jokl (1970) say that fitness is man's

ability to survive under extraordinary demands and
that the size of the physical reserves and general
adaptibility to greater physical demands must be a
determining factor of that physical fitness. This
appears to be a slight shift of emphasis from the
"whole individual" and pure dynamic approaches to
fitness towards the biological/medical model,
although it still suggests that fitness is
multifaceted and environment related.

Bortz (1960) felt that fitness should be defined
in relation to age and normal activity. This,
perhaps, requires bearing in mind when considering
elderly individuals who participate in physical
activity. This approach couples the ability to
respond to life's physical, emotional and social on
going demands with age. A different light is shed on
the concept of fitness here through the involvement
of emotional and social demands. Throughout the
decade (1960-1969) differing concepts of physical
fitness were suggested, indicating perhaps that this
was an era of change in this respect. Cureton (1960)
describes fitness as involving the whole person;
Bruner (1960) suggested it was man's ability to
survive under extraordinary demands. In 1965 Holding
described fitness as the ability to perform daily
tasks with no undue stress or stain at the end of the
day, but does not mention the whole individual.
Holding (1965) considers fitness in relation to the
necessary overall output of effort over a period of
time (in this case a day) rather than single isolated
tasks.

By the beginning of the 1960s, it appears that
the wholly medical/biological concept of physical
fitness that was rather idealistic had, in fact, been
superceded by a variety of concepts related to the
total individual, the dynamic concept, the dual
concept of the biological related to the environment,
and the organic approach, few concepts at this stage,
though, are related to the circumstances or daily
tasks which the individual might be involved with.

It is only later, in the 1970s, that the
understanding of fitness, not only in relation to the
elderly but also to the total population, has shown a
continual development towards the dynamic model that
is also related to the circumstances of the
individual and the daily asks she might be called
upon to undertake. Although the medical/organic
model is inherent in this approach to physical
fitness, it is not the central core of the positive,
multifaced approach of the dynamic concept that
appears to be to the fore at the close of the 1970s.

There appears to be, though, a need for research into concepts of physical fitness as understood by specific sections of the population (e.g. the elderly). For it is only when such concepts are known, compared and understood that it will be possible for professionals who work with specific elderly groups to offer advice in the form of Health Education on how to maintain or improve fitness that is meaningful, comprehended and thus acted upon. The professional and voluntary groups who work with the elderly must also take cognizance of any developments in the understanding of physical fitness if they are to make a valid contribution to communicating of new concepts to their clients through the medium of Health Education.

Cognizance of the development from the medical/biological concept of physical fitness to the variety of concepts related to the total individual in her particular circumstances together with the daily tasks she might be called upon to undertake should be reflected in reports, directives, and work procedures of the many professional groups.

It would appear that as the concepts of fitness have evolved during the past two decades to the whole individual, so too have the Health and Social services. This has brought about greater consideration of the individual elderly person in her own situation. The trend to encourage Health and Social Service workers to keep the elderly in the community rather than institutionalising them has evolved throughout the 1970s. This has involved the Social Services not only in considering the necessary support services that might be required but also to what use the many Victorian workhouse relics can now be put.

The understanding of fitness almost twenty years ago looked towards the ability to survive the stresses and strains of the environment as the underlying fitness factor. The Seebohm (1968) Committee saw the need for a unified approach to the provision of Social Services in order that the underlying causes, rather than just the presenting symptoms, might be cured. Similarly, as the understanding of fitness was being related to the community's comprehension of the term a decade earlier, Seebohm (1968) saw one department for Social Services or "welfare" as the community understands it.

Hatch (1978) suggests that the fastest rate of expansion in the social services will be 6% in the increase in Health Visitors and home nursing. These two areas of the Social Services are very involved in work with the elderly in the community. With the changes in the concepts of fitness in relation to the elderly and their ability to be able to function in the community, the Health Visitors and Home Nurses have a vital role to play in maintaining the elderly in society and thus bring Seebohm (1968) to fruition. How far the Health Visitor or Home Nurse does this will depend on her concepts, attitudes and beliefs regarding activity and fitness in old age.

Voluntary and professional organisations show similar increases in the expansion of the home visiting aspects of their work. The voluntary workers may be members of a formal organisation (e.g. W.R.V.S. or B.R.C.S.) or just friends and neighbours. These people provide services that are supplementary to the statutory services, and help promote community understanding and acceptance of health care (Duncan 1978). Voluntary organisations have undertaken similar roles in the community in recent years in relation to the understanding of fitness through the formation of self help groups and street activity groups as illustrated by the results of the Health Education Council "Look After Yourself" campaign in 1978.

As the Administration on Aging (1978) suggested fitness is

> the condition that helps a person carry out his daily duties and responsibilities successfully, and yet have enough resources to enjoy his social, civic, cultural and recreational interests.

The role of the social services have developed in recent years to help the individual to do just this in his own house in the community rather than keeping her in long stay hospitals or institutions where his fitness will deteriorate. Both the voluntary and professional workers have roles to play in this work. As this work has developed the role of the volunteer has been seen as complementary rather than challenging to the role of the professional working with the elderly both in the hospital and the community (Duncan 1978).

Van Meirhaegue (1972) suggests that the improvement in the general health of the elderly is the result of improved health and social services which have raised the physical and intellectual standards of the elderly. This suggested improvement

in general health appears to follow the change in the understanding of fitness in relation to the elderly over recent years from the purely medical to the dynamic model related to the whole individual but it precedes the changes in the health and social services resulting from the 1970 and 1973 Acts of Parliament.
All workers with the elderly, voluntary and professional, are today concerned with the rehabilitation of the elderly and their return to their own environment. Once there the workers concern is maintaining them there rather than institutionalising them. This follows closely the evolution of the understanding of fitness as it relates to the whole person being able to do tasks, and take on responsibilities successfully, while still having energy for other aspects of life, as put forward by the Administration on Aging (1978) in their understanding of fitness.
As changes have occurred in the understanding of fitness during the past two decades, so have come changes in the activity patterns in old age. These activity patterns reflect the changes in attitudes and beliefs based upon the changing perceptions and attitudes of society regarding the role of the elderly in that society. If Health Education advice that is applicable to, and takes cognizance of these changing concepts of and attitudes to activity in old age is to be communicated to the elderly, it is of utmost importance that those members of the Health, Education and Social Services have the knowledge and understanding of these concepts and attitudes within society. Staff must also have knowledge of the changing activity patterns in old age that result from the changing social expectations and the demands required by these activities in order that the elderly can maintain their independence in the community. Some examples of these changing activity patterns will now be discussed in Chapter 2.

TABLE 2.1

Assessment of Fitness in Relation to Blood Pressure

	Systolic B.P.		Daistolic B.P.	
	0-179	180+	0-99	100+
Fit Men	62.5%	57.0%	60.6%	62.0%
Fit Women	57.0%	43.5%	50.0%	44.0%

Source: Hobson, W and Pemberton J. (1955)

TABLE 2.2

Mobility : Fitness : Age

	60-64 years		65-69 years		70-74 years		Over 75 years	
	M	F	M	F	M	F	M	F
% Unrestricted mobility	76.7	81.6	64.8	78.9	43.3	57.3	36.6	
% Restricted outside	16.3	15.8	23.8	21.2	40.5	35.6	41.7	
% Bedfast or housebound	7.0	2.6	11.4	-	16.2	6.9	21.7	
% say feel fit	73.2	66.7	63.9	61.3	36.3	58.6	36.8	
% Doctor says fit	47.5	38.5	27.3	27.3	11.1	18.3	13.6	

Source: Hobson, W and Pemberton, J (1955)

TABLE 2.3

Health Related to Function
(Roscow Scale)

	Function					
	6 (best)	5	4	3	2	1 (worst health)
Health GOOD for age	98	95	85	62	50	33
Women 70-74 years	16	17				19
Men 70-74 years	28	20				11
Women over 75 years	7	9				38
Men over 75 years	21	15				16

Source: Rowcow and Breslau (1966)

TABLE 2.4

Satisfaction with Health

	18-44 years	45-59 years	Over 60 years	All
Male	8.4	7.7	7.8	8.0
Female	8.3	7.3	7.2	7.7
Both	8.3	7.3	7.3	7.8

Source: Age Concern (1977)

22

TABLE 2.5

Fitness and Ageing

	Male					Female					All				
	65 66	67 69	70 74	75 79	80 +	65 66	67 69	70 74	75 79	80 +	65 66	67 69	70 74	75 79	80 +
GOOD															
Denmark	52	55	56	35	62	53	50	48	46	47	53	52	52	51	54
G.B.	61	62	59	61	62	57	58	53	48	55	59	60	55	54	58
U.S.A.	52	56	59	47	51	58	48	51	48	52	56	54	54	46	52
FAIR															
Denmark	30	35	29	31	22	35	33	35	36	33	33	32	32	34	28
G.B.	26	30	27	26	25	28	29	31	37	30	27	29	29	32	28
U.S.A.	28	24	26	34	32	27	34	31	34	27	28	30	29	34	29
POOR															
Denmark	18	14	15	13	16	10	17	17	18	20	14	15	16	15	18
G.B.	13	8	14	12	13	15	13	16	15	15	14	11	16	14	14

Source: Shanas et al (1968)

23

Chapter Three

THE CHANGING ACTIVITY PATTERNS OF THE ELDERLY IN
RECENT YEARS

> Health is understood more in terms of the
> responses or adaptations of individuals and
> their families to particular situations. Much
> thought is given to ways in which a person's
> capacity for active life can be maximised and
> his disability overcome.
>
> (Wilson 1975)

An individual's capacity for active life will
determine which of the many activities of daily
living and leisure pursuits she will undertake. The
activities undertaken will also be predetermined by
the individual's perception of the physical demands
of each of those activities in addition to her own
perceptions of her level of fitness and physical
ability. The way an elderly individual perceives the
suitability of an activity may also be affected by
her interpretations of both social attitudes and
expectations coupled with the Health Education
advice that they receive from the Health, Education,
and Social Services staff with whom they have
contact.

As one ages, individual adaptations are made in
order that activities of daily living, seen as
important to the individual, may be continued.
However, no two individuals will have the same
priorities, nor similar perceptions, for each
individual has her own unique background experience,
current situation, and values.

Bromley (1972) and Cunningham and Henry (1961)
indicate that discouragement is encouraged by social
norms and expectations which affect the behaviour of
the elderly. Bromley (1972) further suggests that
discouragement is further fostered by lack of
mobility, social discouragement reduces the range of
activities pursued and the pressures to conform to
the social norms and leads to an increased

preoccupation with the self (Bromley 1972; Cunningham and Henry 1961). This is very different from the actual findings of Miller (1963) in the rural elderly. Such a theory requires much deeper consideration in light of the many studies that look at activities of the elderly from a variety of perspectives.

Cunningham and Henry (1961) suggest that the decline in the overall interaction with others is significant with age. There is a marked decrease of social involvement approximately five years after retirement. The signs of disengagement include less activity, more sitting down and disenchantment.

Social interactions and interpersonal relationships are often important indicators of a healthy adjustment to society, adequate mobility, and adequate ability to cope with the activities of daily living. (Macheath 1978). Not taking physical activity involving leaving the house during the winter months as suggested by Hazell (1960) very quickly reduces the level of fitness and the ability to cope with less demanding physical activities.

FACTORS AFFECTING PARTICIPATION IN ACTIVITIES

The activities and mobility of older country people are often marred by their tendency to be overdressed - as the weather cools the layers increase (Miller 1963). Miller (1963) feels that the country elderly often taken on far too much, continuing with their many physical tasks (keeping poultry, pigs, tending the garden) which can often lead to a crisis if put before survival needs (cooking, shopping, etc). The daily physical tasks they have always been expected to do have stayed with them alongside their other interests into and throughout old age.'/ In many respects perhaps the ageing countryman benefits from this positive cycle in that the activity involved keeps the rural elderly mobile to be able to perform these activities and thus keep the muscle tone and fitness level high enough to cope.

Weston and Ashworth (1963) suggest that going out depends on interests and activities coupled with good physical and mental health. However, this is a rather idealistic approach, for many elderly have a low level of physical health and mobility but can certainly still get out and about to enjoy an adequate social life.

The life time habits of the elderly play an important role in the current social, physical activities of these individuals (e.g. visit the pub, get the bus into town). Such physical and social activities provide the social contacts and mental stimulation as well as encouraging the elderly to get out of the house and maintain their level of mobility and fitness in order to continue in other such activities also. They need to be encouraged to continue all these activities as long as possible to maintain fitness and mobility levels, or regain them following illness or injury.

Mobility is the most highly prized quality in old age (Miller 1963). Mobility, freedom, and independent movement are of utmost importance to the elderly if they are to be active and mobile in their communities (Miller 1963). However, Rose and Petersen (1965) remind one that health status influences not only the degree of mobility but also the amount of possible community participation. This will also have an affect on association with other members of society and influence social adjustment. Anderson (1955) listed restrictions on activity due to physical ill health as a major cause of unhappiness in the elderly leading to individuals having few interests outside the home.

Many factors have been suggested as affecting mobility - chronic illness (Arkley 1964); foot troubles (Townsend and Webberburn 1965); osteo-arthritis, shortness of breath, vertigo, impaired vision, and fear of falls (Miller 1963). Goldberg (1970) found that 19% and 20% of those aged seventy plus years and eighty plus years respectively had poor mobility. Sheldon (1958) over a decade previously put the overall figure higher by suggesting that only 70% of the elderly were indeed able to get around as much as they liked and thus enjoyed unrestricted mobility. It is open to question how many of this 70% would get around even more if they had better mobility? Their mobility may be unrestricted in their own eyes because they have drawn in their activities as mobility decrease has crept insidiously upon them.

Ageing leads to a decrease in activities and a decrease in the intensity of activities (Cunningham et al 1968). There is also a decline in group activities (Zaborowski et al 1962). Sidney and Shepard (1977) support this view of activity participation in old age, but take it a stage further indicating that retirement leisure time is filled with physically demanding projects in the earlier years but such activity is less typical in older people.

Some evidence is available (e.g. Szalai 1972) as to how the elderly spend their time both generally and specifically but more age related research is required in order that planning for the ever changing needs of the elderly population can take place.

Most of the studies available have concentrated on urban or surburban rather than rural areas or limited themselves to small areas. Much of the research revolves around the cultural and habitual frameworks and are thus socially determined. Miller (1963) and Griffiths (1958) shed some light on the activities of the rural elderly but there is an urgent need for current investigation and comparison with their urban peers which could prove fruitful and have far reaching effects and repercussions in other aspects of life. Unfortunately the Macheath (1982) also only considers a small area of South East England.

Activities will also be affected the attitudes of the elderly themselves. Bracey (1966) suggests that these attitudes often vary from week to week according to their health and the time of the year. Abrams (1978) reminds one that the elderly are in no way a homogenous group and need considering as individuals.

Participation in activity often involves leaving the home. There is an association between the time it takes to get ready to go out and the frequency of going out (Age Concern 1974). Going out is deterred by the getting ready for many elderly people. Many elderly also do not like committing themselves too far ahead to particular arrangements in case of poor health or bad weather. These aspects can seriously hamper regular participation in many activities involving other individuals especially in the winter months.

Activities of the elderly can be categorised into three main types:
(i)   those of an indoor nature
(ii) those activities involving leaving the house
(iii) those activities concerned with everyday living.

Most elderly people of all ages will be involved in each of the three categories, but the amount of time given to each category may vary according to the time of the year and health status of the individual.

ACTIVITIES OF AN INDOOR NATURE

Indoor activities can cover a vast range from the very passive to the very active, with others or totally alone. Hazell (1960) found that many older individuals did not leave the house for weeks and were cut off from the world. If this is the case two decades later, then indoor activities have a major role to play in the relief of boredom, and the maintenance of a sufficient level of fitness to enjoy the independence and freedom that it has been suggested is so highly prized by these older members of society. Weather may have been a contributing factor in the winter months for older people do not like going out in bad conditions.

In general terms, the elderly appear to enjoy the company of friends and family, indoor hobbies and activities, and looking after grandchildren (DHSS 1978). Moss (1979) considered the total day of the elderly and how the day was divided between the various activities. 66% of the day (16 hours) was spent on family and social interaction, reading, rest and relaxation, and watching television. The more competent read more, especially papers and magazines, and almost 3.5 hours was given to watching the television. From this study, it would appear that the elderly spend a considerable part of each day on these activities all requiring low activity levels of energy expenditure. Many of the activities are lifetime habits as the Age Concern (1974/1977) studies illustrate in Table 3.1 though few appear to enjoy that participation.

In both these Age Concern studies (1974/1977), the elderly are all put into one category (i.e. 60+). The Shanas et al (1968) study illustrates that even lifetime habits are age related with each generation of elderly people influenced by the social and cultural mores of their own formative years.

Watching television appears to decrease with age whilst listening to the radio shows a tendency to increase with age. It must be remembered though, that those over eighty years had sixty years of radio before television was universally available. During the two World Wars (1914-18 and 1939-45) news bulletins were very much part of the daily routine for everyone. These factors are reflected in Tables 3.1 and 3.2 in relation to radio and television habits, particularly in the age related Shanas et al (1968) study. Similarly there seems to be an increase in visits from friends and relations in old age. This requires further breakdown for it could be that concerned relatives are visiting more to provide support services and not friends dropping in for a social chat.

Over 50% of the elderly see their children once a week (Abrams 1978) either by the elderly visiting their offspring or vice versa. Shanas et al (1968) indicate that 37% of the men and 43% of the women have visitors but Age Concern (1974) indicate that only 29% enjoy seeing their visitors. Men are less likely than women to receive visits from friends and/or relations and look forward to seeing them less (Abrams 1978, Age Concern, 1974). In contrast to the Hazell (1960) investigation which suggests that all elderly spend much of their time sleeping in the chair, the more recent studies present a more active image of those over the age of sixty years. Moss (1979) suggests that institutionalised elderly spend twice as much time on rest and relaxation as their peers in the community. If this is so, the institutionalised elderly have much less time to give to the necessary activities of daily living or leisure activities. Do these individuals really require twice as much rest as their community based peers or is this the result of lack of stimulation or provision of suitable alternatives for them? The lack of stimulating and/or physical activities for these people will reduce their fitness levels further and increase the need for support services. Getting ready to leave the institution is in itself physical activity and mentally stimulating however long this takes, and could assist in the maintenance of the necessary base level of fitness rquired for less arduous pursuits.

ACTIVITIES INVOLVING LEAVING THE HOME

Activities outside the living accommodation involve a degree of mobility and strength that is not necessarily required for the indoor activities outlined above. Men appear to be more mobile than their female peers over the age of seventy five years, but until then over 90% of both men and women are usually able to get out and about as Table 3.3 indicates.

Only a very small percentage appear never to go out at all which again illustrates a change from the Hazell (1960) findings of elderly spending long periods of time sleeping in the chair. Activities outside the home may involve the need to be out for a relatively short period of time (e.g. visiting a neighbour) or being out of the house for many hours at a time or even days on end (e.g. eating out; visiting the cinema or Club; having a holiday or break).

Many studies have considered aspects of activities involving leaving the home (e.g. Age Concern 1974/1977); Abrams 1978/1980; Social Trends 1976; Shenfield and Allen 1972; Shanas et al 1968). These studies highlight some of the wide discrepancies in the findings in the overall concept of activity patterns. Again, though, many of these studies consider the elderly as one homogenous group rather than considering categories of elderly people within the vast range that is included in that over sixty years of age group. However, the Age Concern (1974) and the Social Trends/C.S.O. (1976) investigations do relate their findings to specific age groups.

Visiting friends and relations illustrate the wide discrepancies outlined above. The range of 10% to 72% requires further consideration. The earlier studies may reflect the attitudes and concepts of fitness and activity of those days, whereas the higher percentages (72% and 64%) may also reflect the dynamic, whole person in the community approach to fitness in recent years and discussed earlier. Visting friends and relations requires a reasonable degree of mobility and strength in order to prepare for and then leave the home. The Shanas et al (1968) and the Age Concern (1974) age related data highlight a slight decline in these activities with age, but considerable difference between those elderly living alone and those living with other people.

The two Age Concern (1974 and 1977) studies, together with the related Abrams (1978) study, reflect considerable variance in the elderly attending Clubs (30%; 21% and 7% respectively). The Age Concern (1974) data does not reflect the generally accepted norm that more women than men belong to Clubs or that Club membership shows a marked decline with age. However, the 1974 study suggests a considerable increase in Club membership in the 65-69 years age group with the decline in attendance having an effect at approximately seventy five years of age. The data relating to Church and Church activities does not appear to suggest such a decline in participation as outlined above for general Clubs.

Visiting the pub or Working Mens Club does not apparently decrease with age amongst the men but there is a difference between the men and women (Age

Concern 1974). The women in the older age groups would not have frequented such places in their younger days for social mores would have frowned at such behaviour. It is interesting to note the differences in overall visits to these institutions in the two Age Concern (1974 and 1977) studies which are separated by just three years. Similar discrepancies can be seen in these two studies in relation to cinema going and watching sports events. The number of cinema/concert goers is minimal if the Social Trends/C.S.O. (1976) data is meaningful (3% aged 65-69 years and only 1% aged over 70 years).

Approximately one third of all elderly people appear to take a day out occasionally. However, there is no indication as to the type of day out - visiting a place of interest; shopping; Club outing; etc. The means of transport is not given either. Both these factors might affect participation in such activities by the elderly. Many such outings are arranged by Clubs and special interest groups for their members and their friends. Further investigation into the source of such outings and the participants characteristics would give a much clearer indication.

Throughout consideration of Tables 3.1-3.5 one is constantly aware of the varied data for all these activities involving leaving the home. In most cases, though, lack of age related data makes consideration of the vast range of elderly individuals impossible. Another aspect that appears to be similarly scant in detail is the relationship between male and female. Those living alone are often less involved in such activities than those living with others (Shanas et al 1968; Cumming and Henry 1961) but there appears to be little supporting evidence in any recent study (e.g. Age Concern 1974 and 1977; Abrams 1978; Social Trends/C.S.O. 1976).

Moss (1979) found that independent elderly in the community appeared to spend less time with friends than those in aged housing. She suggests that those in aged housing spend approximately three and a half hours each day outside the living unit but the more competent were away longer than their less competent peers. Those in aged housing may well count the majority of their peers as their friends whereas those in the community differentiate between their friends and neighbours. Further investigation is required to substantiate these points.

Abrams (1978) offers an insight into a few aspects which could reflect in the diversity of the findings in several cases. He suggests that 80% of the Club members are female; most live alone; 46% of those aged over seventy five years, together with 40% of those aged sixty five years to seventy four years, are not interested in joining any Club and less than 13% of the elderly belong to any form of Club at all. Similary, the Age Concern (1977) study looks more specifically at holidays (Table 3.4).

With increasing age the tendency appears to be to stay closer to home rather than going overseas. Holidays in Great Britain increase with age, maybe because of the increased problems of obtaining health insurance over the age of seventy five. The small number having a holiday in Ireland may well reflect the concern in the middle and late 1970s at the situation there. Those actually taking a holiday appears to decrease especially over the age of seventy five years.

The Age Concern (1974) study considers another aspect of activity participation outside the home which could add another dimension to any discussion of activities of the elderly and that is regional variation. It is a pity that this data does not relate to age groups and sex to give a more complete analysis of the situation at that time. However, the data in Table 3.5 reminds one that there may be considerable regional variations in and between activities outside the homes. The reasons for this would be many and varied also.

The Club, pub, Working Mens Club etc., are the social centres of the north, whilst the pub is the social centre in East Anglia. East Anglians appear to visit friends and neighbours more than other areas whilst the Church still appears to be the centre of social and other activities in Wales and Scotland. However a closer study is required to consider the similarities and differences between the regions and to look at possible reasons for them before any concrete conclusions may be drawn. For example, the activities of the East Anglians may reflect the transport local opportunities. A day out may be the only opportunity to visit shops in a nearby town. In contrast, Greater London has a much better transport system and travel opportunities and thus one might expect the elderly to be able to get out and about very much more.

Activities outside the home are only possible if the individuals concerned are able to undertake the daily living activities which are necessary preparation to leaving the home (e.g. dressing; preparing meals). Other activities of daily living may be undertaken either outside the home or in the house (paying the rent; bills, etc.). Some of these activities will be considered below.

ACTIVITIES OF DAILY LIVING

If the elderly of all ages are to remain independent in the community, many activities of daily living are essential. However, not all the daily living activities are necessary to the same degree for survival and independence. Approximately 33% of the elderly have some difficulty in carrying out normal activities of daily living (Abrams 1978). The least competent tend to spend more time on their own personal care and less time on household tasks (Moss 1979). This may ultimately affect their continued independence in the community for household tasks do include the purchase of food and also meal preparation. Meanwhile, those in their own homes spend more time on housework, but in general terms older elderly find these tasks less meaningful than discretionary activities.

Again, it appears that there is a discrepancy in the findings related to the activities of daily living in the decade 1968-1978 regarding the elderly. These findings parallel those relating to the activities outside the home, discussed above, as Table 3.6 illustrates.

The only areas where there appears to be consistency between studies is meal preparation. A large number of elderly people indicate that they can still undertake such an important aspect of their survival in the community. It would be interesting to investigate further the nature of such meal preparation for these responses may mean anything from getting out a loaf of bread and a jar of jam to preparing and cooking an excellent five course meal.

Those studies which ask specific questions regarding the activities (e.g. Shenfield and Allen 1972 (1); Shanas et al 1968 (5)) present considerably lower responses than those presented in a more general way (e.g. Age Concern 1974 (3)). A closer study of those doing their own shopping will illustrate this point. Shenfield and Allen (1972) suggest that only 33% in fact do their own shopping. This is supported by the Shanas et al (1968) age-related data: 65/69 years: 40%; 70/74 years: 47%; 75/79 years: 37; over 80 years: 34% ALL: 38%.

In contrast Age Concern (1974) indicates that 80% of the elderly do their own shopping. The Shanas et al (1968) study enquired about just the previous day for which there might be excellent reasons for the elderly individual concerned not shopping (e.g. being early closing day; being the day prior to or following pension day; being very wet or very cold). The reverse is the case though when those living alone in the Age Concern (1974) and Shanas et al (1968) responses regarding 'doing their own tidying daily' are considered. 76% of the former and 97% of the latter responded positively.

In addition, the Shanas et al (1968) study illustrates the steady decline in doing ones own shopping with age, which is not apparent in the other studies. Details of this nature are very essential if the planning of services for the very diverse group labelled "the elderly" are to be pertinent to their needs especially in those areas that are essential to survival and independence in the community.

The personal activities of daily living also need consideration for many elderly individuals have real problems with many of them. These problems often result in their inability to perform the activities outlined above as necessary for survival (e.g. food purchase and preparation). Two of the most crucial personal activities in this respect perhaps are the ability to get dressed and the ability to care for the feet for these are essential aspects of getting out of the house and to the nearest shops. For example, Shanas et al (1968) indicates that 3% of the men and 18% of the women have problems with these two activities and have no one to hand to assist them. Another 10% and 33% respectively have some difficulties with these tasks (Shanas et al (1968). The Age Concern (1974) study suggests that 2% and 22% respectively are unable to dress and cut their toe nails. It appears that there has been little change in these problems for elderly people in the intervening years between the two studies. If these findings remain constant in the years to come more and more elderly people will become housebound and immobile, dependent on others for their foodstuffs as the number of elderly increases.

In his study of two decades ago Miller (1963) found that 92% of his elderly population of country folk were directly concerned with agriculture. He suggests that on occasions, the elderly had too much to do tending their chickens, pigs, etc. and tending their gardens. Problems arose when these chores and the essential household chores (getting water or emptying closets) took precedence over the shopping for food and meal preparation. Rudd (1966) on the other hand, took a very different stance in

34

suggesting that elderly men and women overeat, smoke, drink, and under exert themselves, spending their time and energy on things that were totally irrelevant to their current situation because they cling to the past and their habits of the past. There appears to be very little support for the Rudd (1966) findings in more recent studies. Sidney and Shephard (1977) though, indicate that women spend more time than their male peers doing physical tasks and less time sitting or sleeping. On retirement most of the women's household tasks still have to be done whereas the men had fewer such activities to keep on into and throughout retirement.

If those in the Health, Education, and Social Services who work with this very diverse group of people within the community are to understand them and their needs, it is apparent that detailed research into their activity patterns and attitudes and beliefs is urgently required. Without such knowledge, those working with the elderly are unable to offer suitable positive Health Education advice that will be meaningful to each and every recipient in terms that they will all be able to comprehend and act upon.

Much of the data that is currently available to these individuals provides only part of a very general picture on which to base work with the elderly and the levels of fitness required by the elderly to perform the activities of daily living and leisure time activities both inside and outside the home. Much of the very general data that is available embodies everyone over the age of sixty years. To base suitable advice and information on knowledge that spans thirty to forty years (i.e. sixty years of age through to ninety or one hundred years of age) is not possible. This situation can only be rectified by further detailed investigations of current activities of the elderly utilising much narrower age bands (e.g. five year spans). In the absence of such suitable data for those offering guidance and advice to the elderly, they will draw on their own beliefs and attitudes which may be very different to those of their elderly clients.

TABLE 3.1

Activities by Age

	[1] 18-44	[1] 45-59	[1] 60+	[2] 60+
Watch television	90	93	91	25
Read newspapers	71	82	91	13
Read magazines	67	58	56	
Read books	39	38	39	
Resting	64	72	80	
Knitting etc	32	35	29	12
Having friends/ relatives in	32	36	37	29
D.I.Y.	20	17	18	
Cards/Games	16	9	13	

[1] % participating 1 hour/day in activities by age
[1] % enjoying activity

Source: (1) Age Concern (1974)
(2) Age Concern (1977)

TABLE 3.2

% Living alone and activity the previous day by age

	65-69	70-74	75-79	80+
Watch television	45	41	34	23
Listen radio	62	67	65	69
Have friends relatives in	42	34	41	53

Source: Shanas, E et al (1968)

TABLE 3.3

State of Mobility by Age and Sex

	60-64		65-69		70-74		Over 75		ALL
	M	F	M	F	M	F	M	F	
Usually go out		94	91	90	93	85	99	66	84
Go out sometimes									11
Housebound									5

Source: Age Concern (1974)

TABLE 3.4

Holidays by Age and Sex

	45-64		65-74		Over 75		ALL
	M	F	M	F	M	F	
Have had a holiday	62	62	46	47	31	28	58
Holiday in G.B.	76	73	81	83	85	91	76
Holiday in Ireland	4	4	2	3	5	2	4
Holiday abroad	20	23	17	14	10	7	20

Source: Age Concern (1977)

TABLE 3.5

Extremes in Regional Participation by the Elderly

	% Shop	Visit friend/ relation	Club or meeting	Cinema/ Theatre/ Concert	Bingo/ Whist	Day Out	Pub/ Working Mens Club	Church
Greater London		59	27	13			.12	21
South East					6			
East Anglia	89	74		3		41		
South West						38		
East Midlands			27	4		26	23	
West Midlands						26		
North			37		15		22	
Wales	70	55		3				34
Scotland								48

Source: Age Concern (1974)

TABLE 3.6

Activities of daily living

	1	2	3	4
Prepare own meals	80	90	92	91.0
Do own shopping	33	83	75	37.2
Do own daily tidying	75	82	76	
Do regular cleaning	33			
Do own laundry	60	78	74	86.0
Carry own coal	20			92.0
Pay own bills/rent etc	75			
Garden		58	43	43.2

1   % doing things for self
2   % participating
3   % living alone and doing activity
4   % able to do tasks for self

Source: (1) Shenfield & Allen (1972)

            (2) Age Concern (1974)

            (3) Age Concern (1974)

            (4) Hunt, A (1978)

Chapter Four

HOUSEWORK AND SHOPPING

Housework and shopping are two of the major activities of daily living. Both activities can mean very different things to different people according to their perception of the importance of these activities to themselves taking cognizance of their own physical abilities and the physical demands of the activities. The level of participation in these activities in later years of life will be determined to some extent by the habits formed in earlier years, together with the current situation regarding housing, distance from the shops, health and fitness levels, weather, etc. Each individual determines her own routine regarding daily living activities based on a wide variety of factors including past experience and life styles.

Because a particular individual does housework daily or weekly, it does not mean that their shopping habits will be similar for other factors may well determine the pattern regarding leaving the home. The skills necessary to participate in housework and shopping differ widely, as does the necessary level of physical fitness. One can do the housework without having to go through the process of dressing but going even to the local newsagent at the corner demands the level of fitness to get oneself dressed even with the aid of others.

The lifestyle of the elderly revolves around regular routines and daily habits. Individuals become set in their ways as they age. A deeper understanding of these life experiences and socio-economic aspects of old age could enhance the future success of advice given to the elderly by the Health, Education, and Social Services staff.

The current generation of elderly do not generally enjoy the products of modern technology - the motor car, washing machine, spin dryer, dish washer, refrigerator, - which have given rise to a more sedentary lifestyle and with it an increase in coronary heart disease (Yarvote et al 1974). However future generations of elderly will have enjoyed lifelong exposure to these modern conveniences and may therefore be more vulnerable to ailments related to the lessening of physical activity. Because of the differing demands involved, housework and shopping will need to be considered separately before any comparisons can be made.

HOUSEWORK

Housework can mean anything from just flicking a duster across a table to heaving out all the furniture in readiness for a good spring clean. Housework can include a wide range of activities from bedmaking to cooking, laundry to watering the flowers. The emphasis any individual puts on a particular aspect of housework will be related to her perception of its immediate importance at any given moment of time.

Robinson (1977) found that American women over the age of fifty five years spend 133 minutes per day on total housework. This included 64 minutes on home chores; 34 minutes on laundry; and 29 minutes on cooking. However this data gives no indication of how individuals of different ages within this vast range making up the over fifty fives divide their time on household tasks. The Age Concern (1974) study considers those living alone and also men and women separately whilst Abrams (1980) considers the 65-74 years and over 75 years of age groups and men or women living alone. There are differences in approach in these two studies, but the overall results are comparable. Of those living alone, Age Concern (1974) suggests that 76% did housework; 54% spring cleaning; and 92% cooking in the over sixty five years age group. The Abrams (1980) study reported that in the 65-74 years age group 23% received assistance with housework and 10% received assistance wth cooking whilst in the over 75 years age group the numbers rose to 43% and 22% respectively.

Macheath (1982) investigated not the housework actually done but the beliefs various age groups and professions held regarding the housework habits of the elderly. (Figure 4.1).

As Figure 4.1 illustrates, those over the age of sixty years of age believe their elderly peers do housework daily. From 60% at the age of 60-64 years believing this to be the case, the proportion with such positive beliefs increases to 100%, 95% and 70% respectively at ages 65-74 years, 75-79 years, and over 80 years of age. Those listed as under the age of sixty years are all staff who work with the elderly in a variety of situations. The numbers believing that their elderly patients do some form of housework every day vary from as low as 20% in the 30-39 years age group to 50% in the 40-44 and 55-59 years age groups. The beliefs of these workers may well be reflected in the type of encouragement they offer to their elderly patients regarding the resuming of household chores following illness or injury. If the staff do not believe that the elderly do housework to any great degree, they are certainly not likely to suggest this as a means of their patients getting going again or to talk to them about the basic skills involved in such an activity.

How the different professions involved with the care of the elderly view and understand the habits of their elderly patients regarding their housework may give rise to problems and conflicts if the diversity is too great. Macheath (1982) illustrates that there may be some cause for concern in this area when the beliefs of the various professions regarding daily or weekly housework done by the elderly are considered. (Table 4.1).

Virtually all the community related staff believed that the elderly do housework regularly as part of their routine of daily living. However, the beliefs of the hospital oriented staff, who may be said to be the prime movers in the rehabilitation process are considerably lower.

One must wonder what the nursing staff will then offer in terms of advice to patients leaving their care regarding the taking up of housework again. It must be remembered that housework is a global term which includes not only sweeping and dusting but also emptying bins, spring cleaning, polishing and other such tasks. Doing housework can mean either just tidying the living room, or cleaning the house from top to bottom, or anything between. Each individual will determine for herself what the term is to mean on any given day.

SHOPPING

Shopping can be just as diverse in its demands on the elderly individual as housework. Each individual can believe shopping to be something different at different times according to her needs at any given time. On one occasion this can be just nipping to the corner shop for cigarettes or sweets for that day or on another occasion it can mean a well planned expedition to the nearby town for a large shop of groceries, necessities, or luxuries. Research into the actual type of shopping undertaken by the elderly is urgently required if their habits in this very important aspect of daily living are to be comprehended and cognizance taken of them as an aid to activity or rehabilitation.

Several studies have looked at elderly people and their general shopping habits. Robinson (1977) reports that American men and women over fifty five years of age spend an average of 5 and 6 minutes per day respectively on marketing with a further 15 and 10 minutes respectively on errands and shopping each day. Shanas et al (1968) considered the general shopping habits of those living alone related to age and sex. 44% of the men and 39% of the women interviewed had been shopping on the day previous to interview, but there was an overall decrease with age from 40% in the 65-69 years age group to 34% in the over 80 years age group. However, there may be many reasons as to why individuals did not shop on that particular day - the weather may have been bad; it may have been early closing day; it may have been the day prior to pension day; transport may not have been available that day; or the elderly individual may have had another commitment on that particular day.

Age Concern (1974) and Abrams (1980) also consider those living alone, but these two investigations in addition report on those living with others. Age Concern (1974) found that 75% of those living alone shopped whilst shopping was mostly done by the respondent or spouse in 81% of cases in the group that lived with others. This data compares favourably with the findings of Abrams (1980) who suggests that 26% and 48% of those aged 65-74 years and over 75 years respectively receive assistance with shopping. These figures, though, do not indicate whether such assistance was essential or just accepted because it was offered. Hunt (1978) looked more precisely at how shopping was in fact done for elderly people who could still go out themselves. Hence a much clearer picture emerges, as Table 4.2 illustrates. Those doing all the shopping reduce with age, and although more men and women do part of the shopping, there is also a decrease with age. More men than women have part of the shopping done for them by another elderly person in the household. Older men are more likely to have a spouse in a younger age group than women. Very little shopping is done for the elderly by paid assistance or delivery (just 3.2%) whilst 8.8% and 3.9% is done by relatives and neighbours/friends respectively. Hunt (1978) (76%), Age Concern (1974) (81%) clearly suggest that most elderly people do all or part of their shopping whilst Hunt (1978) (38.9%) and Abrams (1980) (37%) concur as to those receiving assistance with their shopping.

Shopping may not involve going out if there is a mobile service, illustrating that perhaps the housebound can have no problems as the Shanas et al (1968) study shows. Miller (1963) raises the problems of the rurally isolated in poor health for this can have an effect on their shopping because of distances involved. These problems can be lessened considerably for many by the efforts of friends and neighbours.

A different aspect of elderly shopping activities is suggested by Elder (1977), herself aged seventy five years, thus:-

> The Old Age Pensioner on a low income exists by hunting around, using cheap food centres, second hand clothes from Jumble Sales ...

To do this demands mobility and a reasonable level of physical and mental health. There are other reasons too why the elderly hunt around. The current generation were brought up to look for bargains, the best value for money, and cheaper foods etc., having been raised in childhood at a time when money was short and families were large. This could be part of their habitual framework and therefore culturally determined rather than indicating that it has in fact been brought about by old age, poverty, or declining financial circumstances. Many elderly individuals are known to save almost everything for the proverbial rainy day whilst currently scrounging around or making do with just the basic necessities.

Snellgrove (1963) suggests that the mobility of the individual determines the amount of shopping managed by the elderly, but this also applies to other aspects of life involving leaving the house. The number of actual shopping trips in a week may be determined by bus and train timetables or by environmental factors - rain, snow, heat, underfoot conditions - or the subjective health feeling of the elderly individual. Pension day is often observed to be part of the habitual framework of the elderly and is associated with a regular outing to the local Post Office and making other basic purchases at the same time.

The shopping habits of the elderly will depend on the type of household, the number of people, whether the individual has access to a refrigerator, whether it is fresh food, dry goods, tinned goods or frozen foods being purchased, delivery day of particular foods to shops, and the immediate needs of the individual or other household members. All these factors are worthy of serious consideration when the shopping done by the elderly is being discussed.

Macheath (1982) investigated the understanding of regular shopping habits of the elderly by age. The majority of elderly people believe their peers do some shopping every day even in the over 80 years age group. This suggests that perhaps 'a little often' describes how the elderly shop. The reasons for this can include a lack of a refrigerator; the inability to carry heavy loads; the meeting of shopkeepers every day and talking to others; the social need to meet others; habits of yesteryear; etc. Such beliefs indicate a very strong tie to the maintenance of freedom and independence of the elderly generally in the community. In contrast, very few of the staff who make up the lower age groups in Figure 4.4 believe that the elderly shop a little and often. Only in the 50-54 years age group do 50% believe this to be the case. The level of such beliefs drops to 15% and 23% respectively in the 30-34 years and 35-39 years age groups.

The beliefs of these staff that many elderly people shop just once a week may well be tied to the idea that pension day is the one occasion that these people actually go out into the community. It is apparent that many staff believe that quite a number of elderly people do not shop at all in contrast to the elderly who believe that their peers in fact shop daily or at least once a week, as Table 4.3 illustrates.

Only staff in the 50-54 and 60-64 years age groups hold beliefs similar to those of the elderly individuals who will be their patients. When the various professions are considered, again the hospital orientated staff (SRNs, SENs, Nurse Aides) caring for the sick elderly believe this group of older people shop once a week to a much lesser degree than those more community related staff. It is interesting that Age Concern staff do not totally agree with their elderly recipients that they regularly shop and get their pensions once a week.

(Figure 4.3).

If teams of staff in the rehabilitation/support services are to be successful in their work with the elderly as individuals within this very diverse group that make up the elderly, it is of utmost importance that their goals are understood and worked towards in similar ways by every member of that team holding similar beliefs of what the elderly person is capable of and her understanding of housework, shopping, and other activities of daily living. This does not appear to be possible at the present time with such divergent views and beliefs between the many professions regarding just these two basic daily living activities of housework and shopping.

If professional staff do not seriously believe that the elderly do housework or go out shopping on any regular basis one wonders how they believe this sector of the population survives at all. It is surprising to think that staff involved in the caring professions can be so unaware of the elderly and their current lifestyles, or the way the elderly see their lifestyles when they are so closely concerned with these individuals. One wonders how often the staff chat to their elderly patients to find out their habits, beliefs, and views on the basic survival activities in order to then offer advice and encouragement that is appropriate to the individual situation and lifestyle.

FIGURE 4.1

% Understanding of Housework Daily or Weekly
in Old Age by Age**

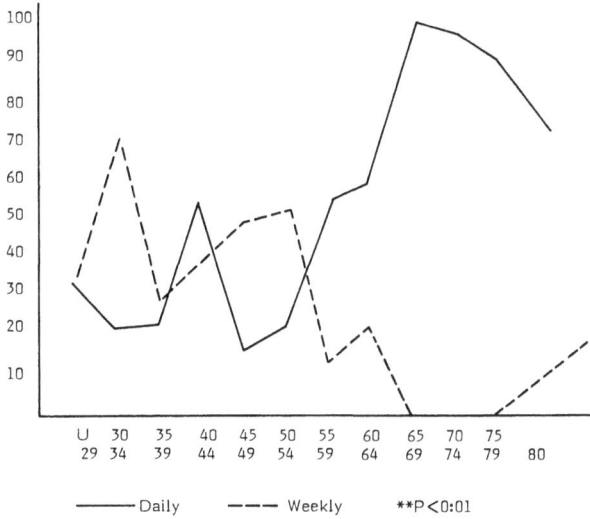

———— Daily   ———— Weekly   **P<0:01

FIGURE 4.2

% Understanding of Shopping Daily or Weekly
in Old Age by Age**

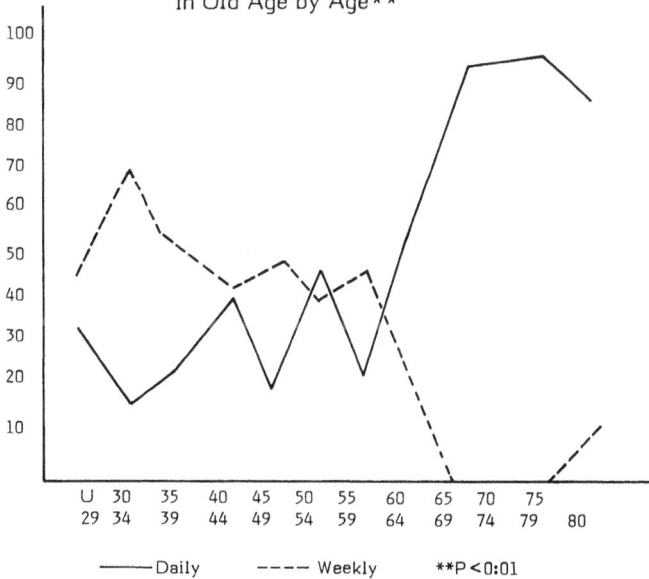

————Daily   ———— Weekly   **P<0:01

FIGURE 4.3

Beliefs of Weekly Shopping by the Elderly
by Professions

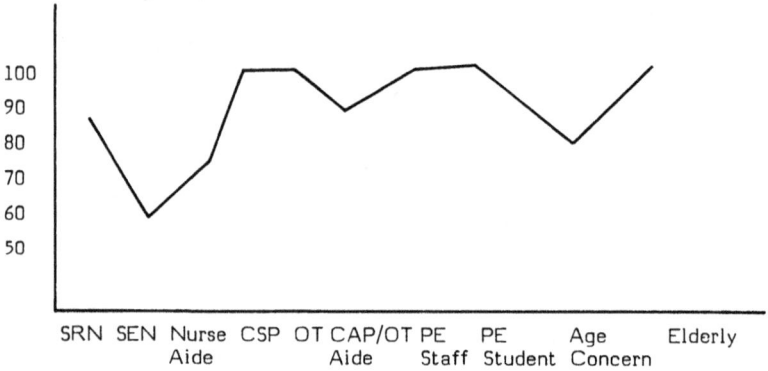

```
100
 90
 80
 70
 60
 50

     SRN SEN Nurse CSP OT CAP/OT PE    PE     Age     Elderly
             Aide          Aide   Staff Student Concern
```

TABLE 4.1

Beliefs Regarding Daily or Weekly Housework
Habits of the Elderly by Profession

SRN	83%	CSP	100%
PE Staff	100%	Elderly Staff	70%
SEN	63%	OT	78%
PE Student	100%	Nurse Aide	63%
CSP/OT Aide	90%	Age Concern Staff	100%

Source: Macheath, J A (1982)

48

TABLE 4.2

How Shopping is done for Elderly Persons able to get out
(by age within sex)

	Grand Total %	Men Total %	65-74 %	75-84 %	over 85 %	Women Total %	65-74 %	75-84 %	over 85 %
Informants do									
All the shopping	37.2	20.9	18.9	27.5	17.4	48.1	53.8	40.8	19.2
Part of the shopping	38.9	44.9	47.5	34.6	23.9	34.8	37.3	30.8	26.7
None	23.6	33.9	32.3	32.9	56.5	16.7	8.4	28.1	54.2
Not stated	0.4	0.3	0.4	-	2.2	14.0	15.0	13.0	-
Part or all done by									
Other elderly person	32.2	43.2	44.1	41.6	34.8	24.8	28.0	19.3	15.8
Other person(s) in household	18.8	28.3	32.6	16.0	21.7	12.4	9.3	16.2	28.3
Persons outside									
Duaghter in law	6.0	4.2	2.9	7.6	6.5	7.2	4.2	11.7	19.2
Other relative(s)	2.8	3.3	2.4	2.5	4.3	3.2	2.2	4.5	6.6
Neighbour/friend	3.9	2.4	1.4	4.2	13.0	4.9	2.5	8.8	13.3
LA Home help	2.0	1.2	0.7	2.0	6.5	2.5	2.1	2.9	5.8
Other paid help	0.4	0.5	0.4	1.1	-	0.3	-	0.5	2.5
Delivered	0.8	0.3	0.2	0.6	2.2	1.0	0.7	1.4	3.3
Other not stated	1.1	1.0	0.8	2.0	-	1.2	0.7	2.4	0.8

Source: Hunt, A (1978)

TABLE 4.3

Beliefs of the Shopping Habits
of the Elderly by Staff Age

	U29	30-34	35-39	40-44	45-49	50-54	55-59	60-64
Daily	30	15	22	42	24	55	25	62
1/Week	44	72	58	42	58	44	55	28
TOTAL	74	87	80	84	82	99	80	90

Chapter Five

SOCIAL ACTIVITIES

Social activities include many and varied types of involvement with others which can be pursued both inside and outside the house. Such activities can involve considerable energy expenditure or very little use of energy; great expense or no expense; both men and women or just men or just women; the elderly individual alone or other family members. These, and other, factors might have a major influence on the social activities of any particular elderly individual. As Bracey (1966) suggests, the situation may change from one day to the next, week to week, or even season to season.

Many elderly turn their hand to voluntary work if they are mobile and in reasonable health. Hinds (1973) indicates that these activities are therapeutic agents in solving many of the personal and social problems of retirement. The voluntary work available varies from one area to another according to the local authority regulations. Meals on wheels and Lunch Clubs in many areas are manned entirely by elderly volunteers whilst in other areas these services must be undertaken by paid employees. Many individuals join Clubs on retirement as a means of continuing to use their work skills and business acumen or are involved in hospital work for the same reason. All these activities also have important social connotations for the elderly participants.

Club attendance, visiting friends or relations, visiting a pub or Working Men's Club, eating out and taking an occasional holiday are all forms of social activity which involve leaving the home for varying lengths of time with or without others. These activities also involve contact with others either individually or as a member of a group.

CLUB ATTENDANCE

Club attendance can involve a regular weekly, fortnightly, or monthly commitment or just an occasional meeting for those concerned. The Clubs may be of a very general nature with a bias to the social aspects of such a gathering; of a more specialist nature involving people with a special interest; or related to the place of worship and for convenience named Church Clubs.

Age Concern (1974) suggests that 34.0% of elderly people belong to Clubs but that 40.0% say they would not enjoy belonging to such institutions. However, Abrams (1980) suggests that only 13.0% belong to Clubs with only 7.0% of socioeconomic classes AB belonging, increasing to 15.0% in classes CD. 6.0% of the Age Concern (1974) sample indicated they had given up attending Clubs. Both these investigations give an indication of when the elderly individuals joined Clubs but consider the data from different viewpoints. 26.0% joined Clubs between the ages of sixty one years and seventy four years of age whilst 11.0% joined after the age of seventy five years (Abrams 1980). In both groups there is an increase in the lower socioeconomic groups. Groups AB tend to join Clubs early in life whilst DE join Clubs after the age of sixty years. This may well reflect the work roles of the various groups for AB are more likely to have the time available to participate in such membership whereas DE are more involved in earning to survive. Club attendance appears to vary in different parts of the country - North 37.0%; London 27.0%; East Midlands 27.0%; Scotland 26.0% (Age Concern 1974). The age of joining different types of Club also appears to vary. Age Concern (1974) indicates that 41.0% join Clubs for the Elderly; 35.0% join Special Interest Clubs; 25.0% Church Clubs; and 9.0% other Clubs before retirement. The corresponding figures for post retirement joining of Clubs were 36.0%, 15.0%, 8.0% and 2.0% respectively.

Bracey (1966) suggests that every area and neighbourhood would benefit from a well organised Pensioners Association centre where all types of assistance and advice would be available over a cup of tea. Age Concern has many such centres today (e.g. Ramsgate, Kent) but there is a need for an expansion of these centres throughout the country. Most of these centres are managed by the elderly themselves and the successful ones are social centres rather than office premises.

Arkley (1964) suggests that a further 23.0% of the elderly would join Clubs if they had the means to get there. Perhaps this information throws some light on the Age Concern (1974) figures of 40.0% would enjoy going to a Club but in fact only 14.0% actually attend a Club. This same study suggests that clubs for the elderly are much more popular with those in poorer health, older women and social classes C2, D, and E.

GENERAL INTEREST CLUBS

General Interest Clubs are social in nature; meet regularly; and involve a variety of activities over a period of time. The most well known of these types of Club are probably the 'Old Folks Club', 'Senior Citizens Club', or 'Silver Thread Club' for the elderly. Data regarding attendance at such Clubs paints a very diverse image within the different elderly populations.

Shanas et al (1968) considered membership rather than regular attendance at Club meetings. Of those actually belonging to 'Old Folks Clubs', 85.0% of the men and 87.0% of the women have relatives and had seen them during the week prior to interview. Only 1.0% and 3.0% of the men and women respectively belonging to this type of Club had no relatives. Having Club membership does not mean that one actually attends with any regularity. Attendance at meeting would give a more realistic picture of the social habits of the elderly. Abrams (1980), Age Concern (1974, 1977), Hunt (1978) and Macheath (1982) all consider Club attendance on either a weekly, fortnightly or monthly basis highlighting many aspects of such activities.

Age Concern (1977) includes all the elderly in the over sixty years age bracket which does not reflect the changes throughout old age. 18.0% of this vast age group attend such Clubs 2/3 times each month in contrast to 21.0% of the 45-59 years age group and 24.0% of the 18-44 years age group. This is in contrast to the Age Concern (1974) study which indicates that 24.0% of women and 20.0% of men aged over seventy five years had attended a Club meeting during the two weeks prior to interview. In the 65-69 years age group the figures are 36.0% and 39.0% respectively for women and men. The Hunt (1978) data presents a different image again, suggesting that in the 75-78 years age group 8.8% and 15.8% of the men and women respectively attend a General Interest Club once a week and a further 2.3% and 3.0% respectively attend such Clubs once a fortnight. In the 65-74 years age group 6.0% of the men and 14.9% of the women attend once a week with a further 1.5% and 3.0% respectively attending every other week. Perhaps the socioeconomic breakdown of Abrams (1980) will throw some light on the makeup of the Hunt (1978) and Age Concern (1974) populations for this study illustrates considerable difference in the weekly attendance. Only 16.0% of socioeconomic groups AB attend Clubs weekly whilst 76.0% (C1), 82.0% (C2) and 85.0% (DE) attend regularly each week.

Macheath (1982) indicates that there is a marked increase in regular Club attendance during retirement then a marked decrease at aged over eighty years, namely:

60-64	65-69	70-74	75-79	Over 80
60.0%	73.0%	83.0%	90.0%	45.0%

In contrast to the Age Concern (1977) study, Macheath (1982) suggests that very few of the young age groups attend General Interest Clubs. Only 4.0% of those aged 30-44 years appear to attend such Clubs.

It is apparent that when General Interest Club attendance habits of the elderly are considered, there is much conflicting evidence available. Each study must be considered in relation to the specific questions being addressed. The Club habits of the elderly appear to be related to age and socioeconomic status. With the increased provision of special transport by voluntary and statutory services, mobility is not the prime factor in Club attendance that it may have been in the earlier studies.

CHURCH CLUBS

Clubs related to places of worship may meet for many different purposes from the deeply religious to the purely social. Differentiation between such activities is not possible, or indeed available.

Age Concern (1974) indicated that just 9.0% of the elderly belong to such Clubs of which only 8.0% had joined since retirement. Abrams (1980) suggested that 13.0% belonged to Church based Clubs which socioeconomic groups AB joined early in life but groups DE joined later in life.

Macheath (1982) found that those attending Church related Clubs were mostly in the older age groups (7.1% aged 30-44 years; 4.3% aged 45-64 years; and 89.8% aged over 65 years). Those over sixty five years of age appear to be evenly divided between the age groups (Table 5.1).

It can readily be observed that in the older age groups Church Club attendance declines steadily with age. Only 2.0% of elderly with no relatives belong to Church Clubs whereas 81.0% and 85.0% of the elderly men and women who saw relatives in the week prior to the Shanas et al (1968) interviews belonged to a Church related Club. Belonging though does not automatically mean attendance. Age Concern (1974) data compares favourable with the Macheath (1982) study indicating that little change in the ensuing eight years of the Church Club attendance habits of the elderly, but they do indicate a difference between the male and female habits. For example, in the 65-69 years age group 33.0% and 24.0% of the women and men attend Church Clubs, but these figures drop to 28.0% and 22.0% respectively in the over 75 years age group (Age Concern 1974).

SPECIAL INTEREST CLUBS

Special Interest Clubs may not meet as often as the General Interest or Church Clubs, but regular attendance occurs nontheless. 12.0% of the Age Concern (1974) elderly sample attended such Clubs of which only 15.0% had joined since retirement. However, Macheath (1982) states that there is an increase in Special Club participation in the 65-69 years age group followed by a gradual decline with age. There is no information available as to the nature of such special Interest Clubs.

Comment

Some general overall trends regarding Club attendance by the elderly do emerge. Many elderly people appear to belong to some type of Club and do attend regularly. Many elderly individuals belong to more than one type of Club. More elderly belong to Clubs than those in the 18-59 years age groups in all three categories (General, Church and Special Interest Clubs), but this attendance decreases gradually throughout old age. However, Macheath (1982) clearly shows that more of the very old in the over 80 years age group than in the under 60 years age groups are still actively involved in Clubs, especially those related to places of worship.

(Figure 5.1).

In general terms the staff working with the elderly do not believe their patients regularly attend Clubs of any sort. Less than 30.0% of the SENs, Nurse Aides, Occupational Therapists and their aides believe the elderly regularly attend such institutions. In contrast over 80.0% of the Physical Educationalists and Age Concern staff believe the elderly regularly pursue such social activities. It is the hospital-related staff, who are involved in the primary stages of rehabilitation, who perhaps need such an understanding of these social activities in order to motivate their patients initially towards picking up the threads of life in the community once again.

Elderly Clubs are a well established part of most communities, providing a raison d'etre for many elderly individuals to get dressed up to go out and socialise with their peers. In order to attend any type of Club the elderly are involved in several activities: preparation; planning ahead; regular commitment involving others; meeting a specific time schedule; decision making and many other mental skills. In addition physical skills are used to advantage through a number of activities: changing clothes; putting on outdoor shoes, coat and hat; ensuring hair is tidy and the women have their make up applied; walking to bus, car or Club; managing curbs, stairs, ramps etc. Upon arrival the social skills come to the fore through greeting; concern for others; conversation; having tea and biscuits; paying dues; taking part in meetings; greeting and thanking speakers, etc. etc. A few of the elderly are able to continue to utilise skills learned and developed earlier in life through participation in the organisation and management of Clubs of all types. Other elderly taking on lesser tasks fulfil their need to be wanted or serving others, whilst the majority of elderly individuals, both men and women, are happy to be just regular attenders.

Clubs for the elderly, regardless of the type, can be seen to provide many hidden benefits for those wishing to participate. Mental, physical, and social skills all readily deteriorate if permitted to go unused and unstimulated just as fitness declines just reclining in bed or sitting in a chair. As the elderly slow down, the preparation, planning, and implementing of the Club visit may take a little longer but the benefits will still be gained from the whole undertaking. It is important that the elderly are encouraged to continue with their Clubs

activities into and throughout old age, and more important to pick them up again as soon as possible following hospitalisation, illness, injury, inclement weather, bus or train strikes etc. This remotivation will only occur if everyone concerned with the well being of the elderly in the community, including members of the Health, Education and Social Services, Club Staff, families, friends and peers, all appreciate:
(a)   the benefits to be gained from returning to Club attendance
(b)   the mental, physical and social skills this involves
(c)   the actual and perceived attendance of the elderly at Clubs of all kinds be they General Interest, or particular Special Interest or Church related Clubs.

These Clubs satisfy many different needs for their members including: social contacts, opportunities for self expression, cheap hot meals, a rest and a cup of tea, a meeting place for friends and the need left by retirement. The need for social experience, and interpersonal communication does not abate with age, indeed it may well increase once old age is reached.

It must be remembered though, that Clubs are not for all elderly men and women. Each elderly individual has different needs that will be met in a variety of ways. The fruits of membership for those that do wish to belong though may be satisfying, stimulating and of great benefit.

VISITING FRIENDS AND RELATIONS

Visiting with others can take many forms. It may be just one individual visiting another, or one individual visiting a group of friends and/or relations, or a group of friends or relations visiting, or getting together at, a common place for a particular purpose. Most visiting as such appears to be on a regular basis, although occasional visits to more distant friends and relations also take place. Indeed distance and transport means available may be deciding factors as to when such visits can actually take place. Age Concern (1974) suggests that there are regional variations in visiting patterns on the part of the elderly:- East Anglia 74.0%; London 59.0%; Wales 55.0%.

Hunt (1978) looked at reasons why such visits could not take place between the elderly. Almost as

many did not wish to make visits (27.0%) as those who could not because of their health (28.2%). Another 24.6% felt the distance was too great, but only 1.7% felt that cost was a prohibitive factor. 6.3% said they had no friends or relations to visit and another 4.3% said they were too busy to make such visits. Visiting friends may also be totally different to visiting relatives and be governed by totally different conventions as far as the elderly are concerned. Research during the past decade and a half has viewed these two activities from a variety of standpoints. The 1968, Shanas et al cross national investigation differentiates between visiting friends and meeting them somewhere. 27.0% and 26.0% of those living alone had visited or met friends respectively on the day prior to interview. When age is considered, visiting friends decreases from 32.0% in the 65-69 years age group to 17.0% in the over 80 years age group whilst there is a similar decrease in the meeting of friends (32.0% to 19.0%). Eight years later, Age Concern (1974) states that 64.0% of elderly people had been visiting during the two weeks previous to interview. The Shanas et al (1968) figures only include those who had made such a visit on the previous day and these figures may well have been affected by a variety of factors (e.g. weather, transport available, day of the week, other commitments, etc.). Without such additional data comparison between this and the later Age Concern (1974) data is not possible. However, this study does consider not only the elderly in age related groups but also within those age bands by sex enabling comparison with subsequent investigations to take place. The Age Concern (1974) data illustrates in the 65-69 years age group that 71.0% of the men and 73.0% of the women had visited someone during the previous two weeks, reducing to 53.0% for both men and women in the over 75 years age groups. The Age Concern (1977) information just gives 57.0% of those aged over 60 years visiting friends and relations - a decreasing overall figure of 7.0% in the intervening three years between these two Age Concern studies. Hunt (1978) considered visiting friends and relations as separate activities - 77.5% visiting relatives and 54.9% visiting friends in the over 65 years age group. The Hunt (1978) data suggests that fewer elderly visit friends than actually visit relatives:-
65-74 years 83.6% visit relatives 61.1% visit friends

75-84 years 67.7% visit relatives 44.5% visit friends
Over 85 years 51.1% visit relatives 31.5% visit
friends.

Hunt (1978) considers further the visiting of
relations and gives some details of who is visited by
the elderly. Sons and daughters (37.7% and 43.2%) are
visited more frequently than brothers (20.0%) and
sisters (35.3%) with few actually visiting
grandchildren and other younger relatives. The same
decreases are apparent with age. Most visits occur
regularly on a weekly to monthly basis to both
friends and relatives. Within the 65-74 years age
group socioeconomic groups Cl (26.0%) and C2 (31.0%)
go visiting more than their peers in groups AB
(24.0%) and DE (23.0%) but the reverse is the case in
the over 75 years age group (Abrams 1980).

There is a diversity with age in the beliefs and
understanding of the visiting habits of the elderly.
Few of the 45-55 years age groups believe that the
elderly visit either their friends or relations
(16.5% qne 17.0%) which corresponds to the beliefs
associated with housework and shopping discussed in
Chapter 4. Figure 5.2 illustrates the changes in
beliefs of elderly visiting their friends and
relations with age that continues into and throughout
old age at high level.

Very few of the hospital related staff believed
that the elderly ever visited their friends or
relations (approximately 20.0%) whereas over 60.0%
of the community related staff working with the
elderly believed their clients go visiting (Macheath
1982).

Rose and Peterson (1965) suggest that visiting
friends and neighbours is more important in
influencing contentment and satisfaction of the
elderly than contact with their offspring. However,
this assumes mobility, a low index on the Shanas et
al (1968) capacity scale, and sound health. Many
elderly do not go house visiting but will meet
friends and neighbours at local 'Contact Centres'
over a cup of tea.

Patterns of visiting friends and neighbours may
be culturally determined for it is not 'the done
thing' in some areas and, therefore not part of the
habitual framework. During the war, too, the older
age group would not have gone visiting expecting a
cup of tea because of rationing. Visiting friends and
neighbours, or rather the absence of it, may be
related to health problems (e.g. vertigo) or personal
living problems or the social norm of this
generation. Those staff in the Health, Education and

Social Services who offer rehabilitative advice to
the elderly need to be aware of all the possible
reasons for and against visiting of friends and
neighbours by their patients. Only then can such
activities be used as a medium of physical activity
to assist in the maintenance or regaining of fitness
as a means of continuing independent living in the
community.

VISITING THE PUB/WORKING MENS CLUB

Visiting such places is often a lifetime custom that
is carried into and throughout old age. One can
undertake such an activity with or without
companionship of others, but one does usually require
a reasonable degree of mobility. Working Mens Clubs
tend to be a more northernly institution but the pub
is a regular meeting place, particulary for men,
throughout the country in both urban and rural areas
alike.

Age Concern (1974 and 1977) report on actual
visits to these institutions whereas Macheath (1982)
reports on the beliefs held by society regarding the
visiting habits of the elderly to these places.

The current generations of elderly women would
not have frequented such places in their youth or
indeed throughout their younger adult years for
social mores did not condone such behaviour. These
attitudes appear to be reflected in the Age Concern
(1974) data: 44.0% of the men and 12.0% of the women
in the 65-74 years age group visited a pub/W.M.C. in
the two weeks previous to interview. These
percentages drop to 29.0% and 4.0% respectively in
the over 75 years age group. The 1977 Age Concern
project puts all the elderly over the age of sixty
yeras into one vast category of which 25.0% visited
the pub/W.M.C. on two or three occasions each month.
There were regional variations also:- East Midlands
23.0%, North 20.0. and Greater London 12.0%. 1.0% had
given up such activities because of the health of his
spouse (Age Concern 1974).

Almost all the elderly, both men and women,
believe that their peers visit such institutions
either regularly or occasionally, but the younger
staff who work with the elderly do not share this
same level of belief (Macheath 1982). For example, in
the 70-79 years age groups 85.0% believe that their
peers regularly indulge in such visits and this
figure only drops to 72.0% in the over 80 years age
group. In contrast, only 36.0% of those aged under 30

years and 27.0% of the 30-39 years age group believe that the elderly have such regular pursuits. Such diversities are also apparent between the various professions working with the elderly in a variety of situations. 40.0% of the SRNs, but only 22.0% of the SENs and Aides, over 60.0% of the CSPs and OTs, but only 10.0% of their Aides believe the elderly regularly visit a pub/W.M.C. In this instance, the professionals have stronger belief levels than their less trained Aides and are closer to the belief levels of the community related staff regarding the visiting habits of their elderly patients. (Macheath 1982).

Visiting the pub/W.M.C. requires a minimal degree of strength, independence, and mobility. It has good social and fitness benefits for the participants and much to offer therapeutically to the elderly. However, unless all the staff involved with the elderly in the therapeutic/rehabilitative process appreciate these positive aspects of such activities, and understand the attitudes of the elderly men and women towards them, they will be ignored in the overall rehabilitation of these people into the community following illness and/or injury.

EATING OUT

Eating out involves many of the same basic activities of daily living that are also required for elderly individuals to go shopping; visit the pub and visit friends and relatives. In addition though, society also demands certain codes of conduct regarding the habit of eating in public which are not required by these other activities. Eating out could involve considerable expense which might make it a prohibitive activity, but one can also eat out relatively cheaply if one so desires. The data available does not indicate the nature of the repast indulged in or the type of place regularly visited.

Age Concern (1977) suggests that only 20.0% of all elderly people aged over sixty years eat out even two or three times each month and that a further 37.0% would indeed like to eat out more often. Hunt (1978) says that just 4.8% of all elderly people actually enjoy eating out with many more men than women in each age group enjoying this aspect of socialisation:-
65-74 years 6.2% of men and 3.6% of women
75-84 years 7.0% of the men and 3.7% of the women
Over 85 years 7.3% of the men and 4.5% of the women.

The reasons for these variations need further consideration, but one answer might well be the roles of the sexes in earlier years where the women has always prepared the meals for the man. Thus an older man living alone maybe, would prefer to eat out where he did not have to undertake the necessary preparation of the food, or wash up afterwards. One might expect some correlation between the beliefs and attitudes of the staff in the Health, Education and Social Services who work with the elderly and their elderly patients in their understanding of the eating out habits of the elderly. Alas the case does not seem to be so. One might also expect some correlation in these beliefs and attitudes with those regarding similar activities. In the latter case the same general trends appear to occur according to Macheath (1982) - i.e. a decided increase in the understanding levels at approximately sixty years of age where it is one's peers in question followed by a slight decline with age. The only change to this general trend with regard to eating out is the increase in the older age group where one would perhaps expect a decline. It is very that the younger staff really fail to believe that the elderly participate in these basically socially desirable activities that all involve getting dressed and leaving the house. None of the hospital related staff believe that elderly individuals eat out (Macheath 1982). Almost all the staff sharing the positive beliefs and attitudes with their elderly patients/clients regarding eating out even occasionally are the elderly themselves who service the Clubs etc. (Macheath 1982). (Table 5.2).

HAVING A HOLIDAY

Having a holiday involves much more than any of the other social activities requiring the elderly to leave the home for any length of time and staying away at least overnight. Only 27.0% of those aged 30-49 years believed that the elderly ever actually did such things. In contrast to this though, 93.0% of those aged over sixty years believe that their peers do take any occasional holiday (Macheath 1982). It must be remembered that a holiday could be just a simple weekend visit to relatives involving nothing costwise after being fetched by car to a luxury vacation at considerable expense. There is very little data available as to the actual types of holiday indulged in by the elderly or the cost of

such ventures.
     42.0% of the elderly had not had a holiday for
the past two years (Age Concern 1974). Age Concern
(1974) also found that 51.0% of those aged over 75
years of age and the same percentage of those elderly
in socioeconomic groups DE had not had a vacation for
at least two years. 11.0% of the over sixty years age
group had had to forego a holiday because of lack of
money for such a venture (Age Concern 1977).
     65.0% of all elderly people are always happy to
go on holiday but 12.0% enjoy it though worrying
about being away from their homes (Age Concern 1974).
Hunt (1978) suggests that only 6.9% of all elderly
people actually enjoy their holiday with generally
more men than women admitting this to be the case.
Only 15.0% feel they do not enjoy having a holiday at
all (Age Concern 1974). It would appear that most
elderly individuals, both men and women, enjoy a
change of scenery now and again, but do not wish to
prolong the experience for too great a length of
time.

Comment
Elderly people, men and women, appear to enjoy
participating in social activities and also believe
that their peers also participate in such activities.
It is apparent that the current generation of elderly
individuals see these activities as important in
their lives. However, the younger generations of
staff who work with them do not perceive them as
important in the lives of their elderly patients.
Even those living alone, and highlighted in the
Shanas et al (1968) work, participated in many of
these social experiences regularly. Many of these
social activities have, or could have, great assets
in the field of rehabilitation of the elderly
following illness or injury but these can only be
utilised if the staff understand how the elderly
themselves participate and believe that their peers
participate in these social pursuits. Visiting the
"local" is almost entirely a male activity in the
older age groups, whereas shopping for food tends to
be a more female pursuit. Eating out and taking a
holiday will usually involve elderly of all types,
individually, with spouses, or with groups with other
friends or relations.
     The current generations of elderly have a wide
range of social activities from their lifetime habits
that they have kept up into and throughout old age.
Future generations of elderly may have totally

different social activities based upon their current lifetime experiences which at the moment appear to be very different from those of the elderly today. As one ages, one tends to lose ones friends, relations and close acquaintances. This may well be reflected in the visiting habits regarding friends and relations accounting for the decline in such visits in later old age. This might also affect the other social activities as members of the peer group are reduced in number, particularly in the over 80 year age group. Decreased mobility may be but one factor that affects social activities of the elderly, but there are many others that might make equally valid reasons for elderly individuals not undertaking a particular social activity at any given time, including the time of the year, cost, transport available, the day of the week, previous commitments, distances involved and whether the elderly wish to pursue the particular activity at any given time. Each individual elderly person will need understanding and considering in relation to her own social interests and needs at any given moment of time.

It is readily apparent that the current generations of elderly men and women have maintained their busy way of life into and throughout old age. Habits formed from necessity in their earlier years have stayed with them throughout life. Socialising and chatting in a variety of ways provided them with the necessary relaxation from work at minimal cost in these early days and it is these same traits that are apparent today.

Social activities involve many hidden mental and physical skills as illustrated through the demands of Club attendance by the elderly and thus provide a good means of maintaining, or developing, these skills which are so essential to independent and free living in the community. Many of these social activities occur at regular intervals giving the elderly men and women a regular, disciplined approach to their daily, weekly, and monthly living.

Many of the social activities for older men and women are clearly governed by the social mores of yesteryear rather than those of today. Social activities for these older people also reflect the experiences of yesteryear for living through the two world wars, the depression, and the arrival of all the convenience aspects of life we have come to accept today (cars, planes, buses, washing machines, spin dryers, etc). Everyone is involved in the process of motivation, rehabilitation and the maintenance of independent living for elderly men and women of all ages must understand and appreciate the effects of these past events on the current lives of their patients.

FIGURE 5.1

% Club Attendance by Age

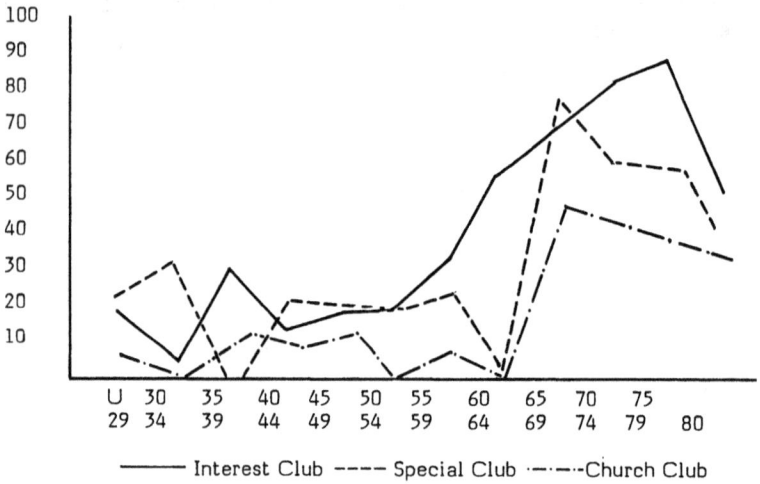

Interest Club ———— Special Club ———— Church Club

FIGURE 5.2

% Understanding of Elderly Visiting
Friends and Relations by Age

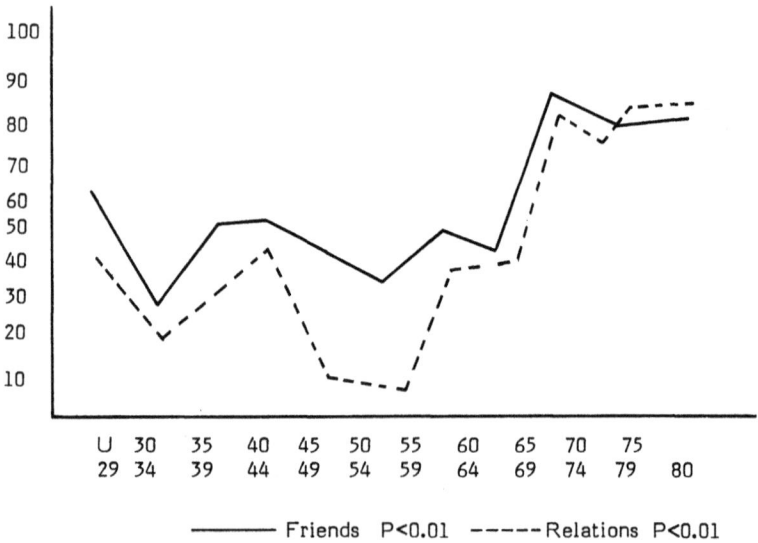

Friends P<0.01 ————— Relations P<0.01

66

TABLE 5.1

Church Attendance by Age

	Regularly	Occasionally	Never
65-69 years	54.0%	4.0%	40.0%
70-74 years	37.5%	10.4%	52.0%
75-79 years	36.5%	19.5%	43.9%
Over 80 years	26.4%	5.6%	67.7%

Source: Macheath, J A (1982).

TABLE 5.2

% Understanding of
Elderly Activities by Age

	Under 40	40-59	60-79	Over 80
Eating out	28	40	84	92
Shopping	22	37	91	84
Visit Pub/WMC	30	34	82	72

Source: Macheath, J A (1982).

Chapter Six

PHYSICAL ACTIVITIES

Physical activities include many of the activities of daily living and social activities involving leaving the home in addition to those more directly concerned with exercise and fitness. However, physical activities also include many forms of activity more allied to hobbies and leisure time pursuits when fishing and other similar activities are considered. Participation in physical activities by the elderly may well depend on whether they see such activities to be sports for the young or general activities for all ages. Participation will also be affected by their attitudes to exercise (see Chapter 8) and their beliefs regarding the effects of such exercise in their own health (see Chapter 9).

The activities under discussion were selected to give a variety of activity, situation and physical demand in order to participate. The activities reflect many activities included previous studies (e.g. Shanas et al 1968) but also includes activities considered to be good all round exercise for all ages (e.g. swimming and walking) and examples of more universally popular activities (e.g. fishing). Included too, are some examples of activities that may require favourable weather conditions (swimming and walking); those that are little affected by the weather and those requiring minimal fitness levels (darts, snooker, dancing). Such a group of activities should include something of interest for most elderly people except, perhaps, the long term bedfast and those in long stay geriatric units.

PARTICIPATION IN SPORT

How individuals actually define sport will determine whether they see themselves participating. To most people, sport involves competition with others in a physical activity of some kind. Participation in different types of sport will vary with age, though some sports may be lifetime pursuits (golf, etc.). The amount of time given to sport may vary with the particular demands of an activity, the season in which it is predominately played, or the arrangement of Club calendars. Many sports do not need Club membership in order to participate (e.g. tennis) whilst others are dependent on such membership and other individuals in order for the sport to be successfully pursued. All these factors take no cognizance of the social mores of the day regarding suitable sports for particular age groups. With the development of Sports Centres in many areas, sports participation has, in theory, become more readily available to people of all classes and ages and abilities.

Robinson (1977) looked at the amount of time Americans spent daily on sport by age which gives a cultural base for comparative purposes. The data illustrates how little actual time this nation devotes to such activities daily (under 30 years - 18 minutes/30-39 years - 14 minutes/40-45 years - 9 minutes/46-54 years - 4 minutes and over 55 years - 6 minutes for men and 3,4,5,0,0, minutes respectively for women). 56.8% of Americans believe the elderly do hardly any sport and a further 28.3% believe they may do just a little (National Council on Aging 1974). This does not paint a very healthy image of the activity habits related to sport of the American nation generally nor of their attitudes to others participating in sports activities (rather than watching the few professional and College athletes season by season).

Age Concern (1977) did not look at the daily sports participation of the British elderly, but at their monthly engagement by age. This study differentiated sport from other forms of physical activities and thus the interpretation of "sport" may well be reflected in the results. 32.0% of the 18-44 years age group participate two or three times a month, but there is what has become the natural decline with age to 8.0% in the over sixty years age group. It is suggested that 40.0% of the 18-44 years age group and 12.0% of the over 60 years age group would like to participate further in sports activities (Age Concern 1977). 6.0% of the elderly had given up participation in various aspects of sport for a variety of reasons - deterioriating health, too old, too tired, etc. - whilst 2.0% had actually taken up an activity and 2.0% looked forward to their future partcipation in sports and games (Age Concern 1974). Abrams (1980) found that 85.0% and 67.0% respectively of those not participating in the over 75 years and 65-74 years age groups were frustrated by physical disability whilst 2.0% and 11.0% respectively said they were too busy to participate in sports activities. In the over 75 years age group 8.0% do more and 53.0% less participating with 16.0% and 34.0% more and less respectively in the younger age group of elderly as compared to what they had done five years previously (Abrams 1980).

It is suggested that physical activity is an essential aspect of health and fitness (H.E.C. 1976; S.H.E.D. 1978; H.E.C./S.H.E.D. 1980). Concern must be raised regarding the communicating of the need for physical activity to specific sectors and age groups within the general population.

The Select Committee (1974) indicates that 33.0% of leisure time is spent watching television, whilst physical recreation occupied 11.0% of male leisure time and 4.0% of female leisure time, but both young men and women name physical activity as their main leisure time pursuit. However, the Select Committee (1974) goes on to say that only 10.0% of adults had actually swum at all in 1965 and only 5.0% had "camped or fished, or played tennis or team games, or been hiking or sailing" during the year. They suggest that sport is concentrated in the under twenty five years age group and declines heavily in old age. It would appear that there is a discrepancy in the 1965 data of this Select Committee (1974) findings and the more recent data discussed below.

Many of the more traditional activities of the elderly are similar to jogging and running activities of the younger age group in that they loosen joints but do not actually increase flexibility (e.g. snooker, darts, bowls). Other activities (e.g. swimming, dancing, tennis, badminton) will both loosen stiffened joints and increase flexibility. Larson and Michaelman (1973) also suggest that climbing stairs, playing golf and sailing are good flexibility activities that will help the mobility of the elderly. These activities become more important as the elderly are more often restricted in participation because of painful joints which result in the further limitation of movement and weakened muscles. Increased activity will improve the range of movements in the joints (Williams and Sperryn 1976). Properly planned and regulated physical activity is one of the most important factors in helping to compensate for physical limitations (Larsen and Michaelman 1973). Woolf (1961) suggested over two decades ago that physical activity and Health Education are the most important and urgent factors in the prevention of disease and the maintenance of fitness in the elderly.

WALKING

The current generation of elderly people over the age of seventy years did not enjoy the luxury of the car, regular transport, buses, trains, etc. in their early adulthood that is readily available today. Travel meant spending money that might well have been required for family food and clothing. Walking was, perhaps, the main method of getting from place to place both in their early years and during the two world wars through which they have come when transport was either unavailable or interrupted. Cars, motorcycles, buses and trains have been the accepted modes of transport for one and all for the past forty years. These factors may well be reflected in the walking habits of people of all ages today for better or for worse. Today, too, walking is seen as a form of physical activity and exercise in the maintenance of health as well as an important aspect of the activities of daily living so necessary for the survival of independence and freedom for the elderly in their communities.

Walking also means mobility and ambulation. These elderly unable to walk any distance may also develop psychological problems and social isolation (Townsend and Wedderburn 1965). Once the ability to walk is afflicted many other health problems develop for every aspect of life is affected.

Many elderly people have trouble caring for their feet (Shanas et al 1968) which will affect their attitude to walking as an activity or a means to an end (shopping) if they have developed painful feet problems. Anderson (1972) stresses the need for screening those aged over seventy years for corns, postural defects and anaemia. The providers of the Social Services need to look hard at the methods available to improve the chiropody services for the elderly for by increasing their mobility and independence this could release money from other, more expensive areas of provision arising from the related foot problems. With well cared for feet and good fitting shoes walking is an excellent physical

activity for the elderly for it has many social and
domestic advantages in addition to the fitness
gained. How the elderly view the need to walk and the
benefits of walking will determine whether or not
they will take a walk for its own sake or not.
Macheath (1978) suggests that the elderly
relate walking to freedom of stiffness and keeping
going. It is also seen as a yardstick of their health
by many elderly people.
Age Concern (1974) reports that 73.0% of older
people walk half a mile a day but also that 5.0% had
given up walking as an activity regularly because of
their health and/or its being too tiring. These
figures show an increase on the Shanas et al (1968)
data of eight years previously - 52.0% of the men and
65.0% of the women living alone had walked on the day
previous to interview - but a slight decrease in
comparison to the Macheath (1982) data eight years
later - 79.2% of all elderly walked regularly.
However, these studies do not use identical
populations and the general inference of the three is
that elderly people do walk regularly in a variety of
situations.
Both Shanas et al (1968) and Macheath (1982)
illustrate that walking does decrease with age whilst
Abrams (1980) indicates that the actual amount of
time given to walking does not decrease with age or
generally with socioeconomic groups. There is no
indication of whether the distance covered, though,
decreases with age indicating that with age the speed
of walking also decreases (Table 6.1).
When the Abrams (1980) data is further broken
down, some information on the actual amount of their
leisure time is spent on walking. Those living·alone,
both men and women, appear to spend longer walking
than those who live with others throughout old age.
Walking gives a reason for being out and about,
seeing other people and different environments.
Elderly individuals may only communicate with the
rest of the community, particularly in a rural
environment, when they are outside the home. Further
investigation of the walking habits of the elderly
may provide some intersting and useful data in this
respect and indicate more socially orientated needs
for walking.
One would expect both the speed of walking and
the distance walked to decrease with the
deterioriation of mobility and health. However, with
the hip replacement surgery that is becoming more
readily available the reverse is also true for many
elderly individuals are now able to walk well again

following a long spell of deterioration is speed and distance.

Walking may be undertaken out of necessity for the elderly, but very often it is coupled with the need to shop, going to a Club, visiting the pub, visiting friends and relations, and other social activities. If walking becomes a problem for any reason at all these other important activities in the lives of the elderly may be curtailed with disasterous results.

The Macheath (1982) data clearly illustrate that the elderly walk regularly to a far greater extent than the younger staff who work with them (see Figure 6.1). A similar disparity can be observed amongst these age groups who indicate that they never walk, except in the over eighty years age group (30.1%). Many of this latter group are long stay hospital patients. The elderly walk where the younger age groups may either go by car or wait for a bus or train to take them. Even in the very old 50.0% walk regularly whereas only 30.3% of the staff under the age of forty years walk regularly. When those aged over sixty years are considered 92.0% aged 65-69 years and 84.0% aged 70-79 years walk regularly followed by a considerable decline once health declines in the very old. (Figure 6.1).

With so few of the young staff walking today there are indications of major problems for those involved in the rehabilitative process when the young move into the older age groups in the 1990s and 2000s. The social mores of today militate against walking when one can go by car creating lifestyles that lack the understanding of the real benefits of walking on health and fitness. If these people do not walk themselves, motivation of the elderly to walk following illness or injury to regain their strength and joie de vie will prove problematical through lack of communication.

Below the age of fifty years few people believe the elderly walk regularly. There is a steady increase with age prior to this time, but then there is a sharp increase in the beliefs level to approximately 75.0% by age sixty five years. Those over this age strongly believe that their peers walk regularly. Only 27.0% think their American elderly peers walk to any extent (National Council on Aging 1974). Relatively few hospital staff, but most of the community related staff, believe the elderly walk regularly (see Appendix B). With so few staff believing that the elderly actually walk regularly it is not going to be utilised or suggested as part of the rehabilitative or resocialising process. It is an activity that can be done in the hospital situation, but this is not likely to occur in this early crucial stage if staff do not perceive it to be a worthwhile pursuit. These differing beliefs regarding the elderly and their walking habits may also have some bearing on the beliefs regarding the shopping and social activities of those same elderly for walking to, such activities are very necessary for the success of them. There appears to be a correlation between actual participation in walking and the beliefs held regarding elderly walking habits on the part of the staff in the under sixty years age group.

It is apparent that the elderly see walking as an important, and necessary, part of their lives whereas the staff working with them do not hold the same view of this basic activity. If the speed of walking slows with age, these other social and physical activities that are crucial to their daily living will take longer. Any decrease in health or mobility that affects walking for the elderly will have a 'snowballing' effect on the rest of their lives, thus the maintenance of walking is crucial throughout old age.

SWIMMING

To participate in swimming requires additional factors - transport, mobility, special clothing, etc. - which may make participation for some individuals impossible or at least very difficult. It is, though, an activity for all ages regardless of ability and physical prowess. The number of swimming pools available have increased considerably throughout the past two decades making this activity more readily accessible to all sectors of the population. Many individuals of all ages swim occasionally when on holiday, especially when holidays are taken abroad in warmer climates. Age Concern (1977) and Macheath (1982) both enquired about the swimming habits of the elderly, but there appear to be few other specific enquiries into such elderly pursuits. 21.0% (aged 18-44 years), 9.0% (aged 45-59 years) and 1.0% (aged over 60 years) swim two or three times per month (Age Concern 1977). The Macheath (1982) study does not find swimming to be a regular activity of the younger age groups. Less than 20.0% of those aged under forty five years of age swim regularly, but from the age of fifty five

years there is a steady increase in swimming until
the age of sixty nine years when 75.0% participate
regularly. This high level drops to 50.0% in the
seventy year olds and to 16.0% in the over eighty
year olds. Although there is the expected decline in
participation with age, participation in this
particular activity is maintained well into and
indeed throughout old age. Swimming being a non
weightbearing activity, taken in a warm climate and
atmosphere, appeals to those plagued with arthritis
and other immobilising conditions and is
therapeutically beneficial to them. This might be a
factor in the high participation levels of the
elderly in the Macheath (1982) elderly.

11.0% of those aged over sixty years felt they
would like to participate more in swimming. One of
the problems of swimming for the elderly appears to
be the lack of age banded sessions for the older age
groups. They do not like to swim in general public
sessions at public pools which are noisy, where they
are likely to be jostled, splashed, and hampered by
the younger users of the pool. Where general sessions
for the retired area arranged they are well supported
by elderly of all ages who are willing to travel long
distances to enjoy participating and its benefits for
their general well being. Many elderly with mobility
problems which affect their walking and hence their
participation in many activities could reap the
benefits of swimming if transport could be made
available regularly to get them to the facilities.

Swimming can also provide the elderly with the
much needed socialising that may have been forfeited
when walking was curtailed. Social mores today do not
see swimming just as an activity for the young, thus
more suitable, and larger sized, swim suits are more
readily available.

From the age of fifty years participation and
belief levels follow similar trends in Figure 6.2
which are well above those of the younger staff age
groups. None of those in their middle forties to
middle fifties swims regularly whilst only 15-20% of
those below these ages do so. (Figure 6.2).

It is interesting to note how many elderly today
do in fact participate in swimming on a regular basis
today, perhaps suggesting pools are more readily
accessible to the older age groups than in years
past. Consideration of the types of swimming and the
ability levels of the elderly would provide necessary
information required for further development of
swimming for those aged over sixty years.

Where such age banded swimming sessions are

available, the elderly readily participate regularly. This is clearly illustrated by the Macheath (1982) study for in this area classes are arranged under the aegis of Adult Education at Nonington College specifically for the retired. All are full and illustrate that there is a demand for such classes. The high figures in this study could be repeated throughout the country by the provision of similar classes and sessions. To date though, the figures in the Macheath (1982) study must be considered as atypical.

Swimming is an ideal activity for the older age group. Being non weight bearing it has great therapeutic value for arthritis, obese and many others disabled through a variety of conditions. These individuals can use this activity as an excellent means of maintaining their strength, mobility and flexibility without the need of sticks, canes, zimmers etc for support.

In light of the high participation levels in the Macheath (1982) District Health Authority by the elderly the high levels of the elderly beliefs that their peers also participate comes as no surprise. They appreciate the benefits of swimming to themselves and this reflects in their overall approach.

One must wonder whether the staff appreciate the particular merits of swimming as a non-weight bearing means of physical activity not only for the elderly but also for themselves.

As highlighted with walking, just 15.0% of the Health, Education, and Social Services staff making up the younger age groups in Figure 6.3 actually believe the elderly swim at all. One must wonder what these staff believe would be suitable physical activity for their elderly patients and what they believe the elderly do with such poor levels of beliefs of elderly participation in walking and swimming. Apart from the 40-49 years age groups the low belief levels of the staff regarding the participation habits of the elderly patients tend to follow their low participation levels.

Believing that the elderly swim regularly is not shared by all the professional groups working with them alike. Only 10.0% of the hospital related staff but 76.0% of the community related staff see swimming as an activity pursued by the elderly (Macheath 1982). The hospital staff, especially the Physiotherapists (only 35.0% believe the elderly swim regularly) and the Occupational Therapists (none believe the elderly swim regularly) have a major role in the rehabilitative process of older people. One wonders what other forms of physical activity are seen as beneficial in such a process if both walking and swimming are not considered elderly participation activities by those involved in the initial crucial stages of rehabilitation.

OTHER ACTIVITIES

Many activities can be looked upon as lifetime activities today for they are not classified as contact/collision sports and as such brief time activities of adolescents and young adults. In general terms, sporting participation shows an increase over recent years (Halsey 1972).

Bowls, until recently, was considered a game for the retired, but dancing in its many different forms and fishing are activities pursued by all ages and classes in society. Snooker, like darts, have come to the fore in recent years through television exposure to become acceptable and respectable pursuits rather than beer hall pastimes for all ages. (Table 6.2).

It is readily apparent that the 30-34 and 50-54 years age groups are almost totally inactive in all these pursuits except a little swimming and walking in the former and walking and dancing in the latter. In contrast, the elderly have a healthy interest in a range of physical activities into and throughout old age, although participation in all physical activities does decline with age into the over eighties. Is the elderly participation the result of these activities being readily available to them or is it the result of these activities being perceived as less physical, more social, and in suitable environments or within their capabilities as suggested later in Chapter 8. Further investigation is urgently required to establish the determinants of such increased participation in these particular physical activities later in life.

Bowls and dancing do not appear to be regular weekly activities except for a small nucleus of younger elderly people. The over 80 year olds do not participate but do believe their peers enter into bowls and dancing. With the increased exposure of snooker and darts on television one might expect an increase in involvement by future generations of elderly people. However the current elderly groups may well be prevented from participating through the absence of access to tables and boards. They are both good activities for all elderly which could well provide steady activity and mental involvement coupled with enjoyable indoor socialising without requiring a high skill level in order to play.

Snooker and darts do not require the mobility of bowls or dancing. Indeed only one other individual is required for match play at all levels. Dancing often demands greater speed of movement, moving in relation to others and music, and a large space in which to pursue participation. These may be barriers to elderly involvement particularly for the older elderly who often enjoy and prefer to watch others dance.

The elderly do not, perhaps, fulfil society's expectations regarding bowls - in that only a few elderly participate regularly. Until recently bowls has often been heralded as the game elderly play on the greens in the summer. Macheath (1982) suggests this is not the case at the present time.

The younger staff of the Health, Education and Social Services who work with the elderly do not appear to have any interest in physical activities on a regular basis. None bowl; few dance; even less play snooker and darts; more swim and just 50.0% walk regularly (see Table 6.2). This presents a very poor image to the more active elderly with whom they work when encouraging them to participate for their own good.

When the participation levels of the staff are considered by their professions (Macheath 1982) the hospital orientated staff are very much less involved than ther community related peers. SRNs swim (28.0%), dance (20.0%) play darts or snooker (5.0%); SENs dance (18.0%) and their aides swim (5.0%) dance (12.0%) darts (4.0%) regularly. In contrast Age Concern staff swim (75.0%), walk (100.0%), dance (15.0%), and Elderly Club staff swim (66.6%), walk (75.0%), bowl (23.0%), dance (15.0%) and play darts or snooker (25.0%).

The understanding of physical activity participation patterns throughout old age of the professional groups working with elderly patients could reflect the mores established in the course of their initial and in service training. If these understandings are too diverse between the various professions conflicts and problems will arise for their elderly patients. Macheath (1982) details the source of some of these conflicts and problems. Less than 20.0% of the nursing staff believe the elderly participate in any of the activities in Table 6.4 except walking which 60.0% SRNs and 20.0% SENs believe elderly do regularly. The physiotherapists all believe the elderly walk regularly and over 60.0% believe they also bowl or dance. However only 35.0% believe their elderly patients swim, play golf, or cycle.

The picture is very different when community related staff are concerned. 100.0% of the Physical Education Staff and 80.0% of the Age Concern Elderly Club staff believe the elderly swim and walk regularly but in contrast just 10.0% and 33.0% respectively of the latter two groups believe the elderly bowl whereas 60.0% of the former group believe elderly bowl regularly.

The overall picture regarding elderly participation in various physical activities indicates that few nursing staff believe this to be the case. The level is higher with the physiotherapist but overall very much higher with the community related staff concerning all the activities listed in Table 6.4

The younger staff, although not participating in bowls themselves do see it as an activity of the older age groups. However in general terms, these staff, in the Health, Education and Social Services do not envisage that the elderly patients with whom they work participate in physical activities to any great extent. The elderly do not share such limited beliefs but rather over estimate the participation habits of their peers.

Comment:
If the under sixty year olds are so inactive now, are they going to take up activities upon retirement without a great deal of positive encouragement which the current generations of elderly have done all their lives? Will the inactive under forty year olds reflect in the activity patterns throughout life? One must wonder at this stage, what plans should be made for these future generations of elderly in order to meet their needs following a totally different, and less active, lifestyle from the present generations of active busy individuals.

The current generations of elderly men and women present an image of busy, participating people with a reasonable fitness level due to their lifetime habits of physical activity through the necessity to walk or cycle in order to travel for work, leisure time pursuits, or socialising with friends or relations. It must be remembered, though, that there is no evidence available as to the actual energy level expended during participation in the various physical activities; the types of activity pursued during participaton; nor the reasons behind participation. Do the elderly consider the fitness factors of such physical activities? Do the elderly participate in order to compete with others? Is the activity pursued merely because it is the one available? What physical activities would the elderly actually like to pursue? Do the elderly want to learn new skills within their chosen physical activity or merely enjoy doing those they have from yesteryear? The answers to these and other questions regarding the elderly of all ages and their participating in various forms of physical activity require urgent consideration if facilities are to be available and preparations made to meet the needs of the ever-increasing numbers of elderly in the over sixty age groups. With the increasing life expectancy, and the increased number of men moving into the older age groups cognizance must be taken of the physical needs if health and fitness is to be maintained well into and throughout old age.

FIGURE 6.1

% Walking Regularly and Beliefs that
Elderly Walk Regularly by Age

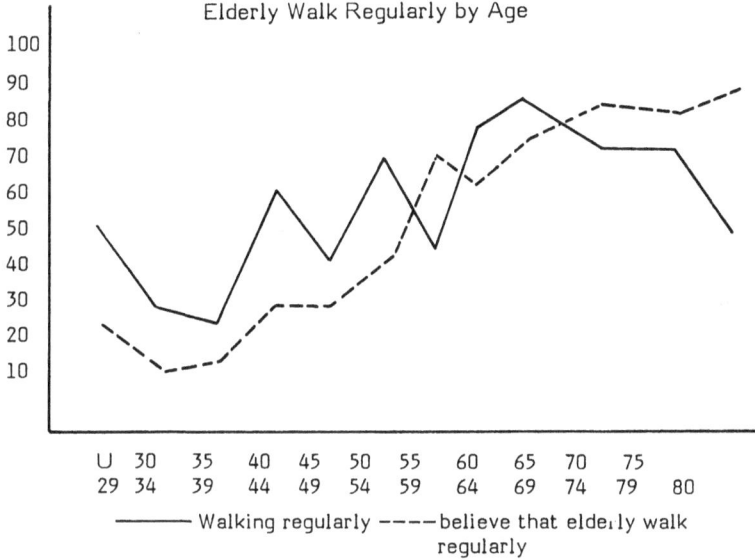

——— Walking regularly ————believe that eldeıly walk
regularly

FIGURE 6.2

% Swimming Regularly and % Beliefs
that Elderly Swim Regularly

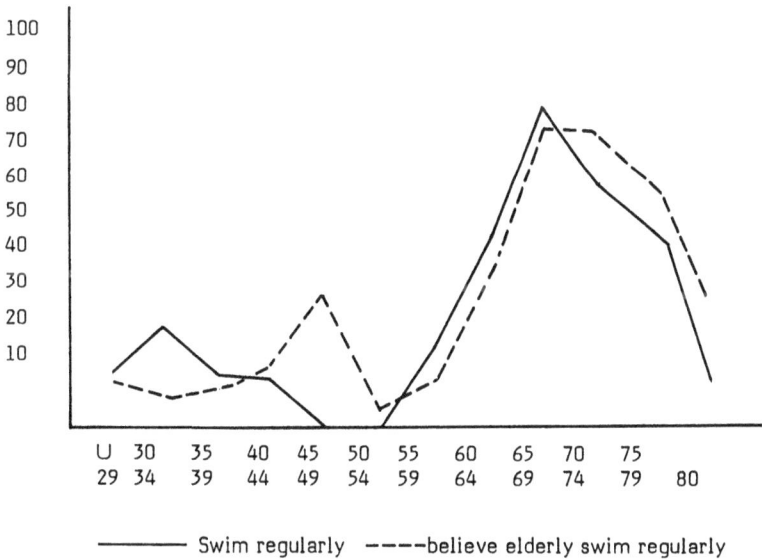

——— Swim regularly ————believe elderly swim regularly

TABLE 6.1

% Walking by Age

	1 Live alone and walk previous day	2 walk regularly	3 hours walk daily
65-69 years	49.0%	95.8%	0.5 hours
70-74 years	43.0%	85.4%	
75-79 years	37.0%	85.3%	0.5 hours
Over 80 years	33.0%	50.4%	

Source:

(1)   Shanas, E et al (1968)

(2)   Macheath, J A (1982)

(3)   Abrams, M (1980)

TABLE 6.2

% Regular Participation in Selected Physical Activities (A) and % Beliefs Elderly Participate Regularly (B) by age

Age	Bowls		Dancing		Snooker		Darts		Fishing		Swimming		Walking	
	A	B	A	B	A	B	A	B	A	B	A	B	A	B
Under 29	0	41	21	48	3	25	9	25	0		18	12	55	30
30-34	0	.54	0	50	0	8	0	6	0		23	8	38	15
35-39	0	42	18	25	0	4	0	15	0		14	12	41	20
40-44	0	64	8	75	0	15	4	25	0		13	18	71	40
45-49	0	30	17	50	0	15	8	23	0		0	40	42	38
50-54	0	80	27	36	0	18	0	30	0		0	6	72	40
55-59	0	72	18	44	9	18	18	33	0		18	15	45	58
60-64	0	100	25	60	13	25	0	28	0		50	50	88	80
65-69	25	100	4	100	21	38	17	70	0		49	78	100	78
70-74	21	100	10	97	19	60	21	100	6		56	80	92	93
75-79	15	100	10	94	15	35	15	55	5		46	67	91	100
Over 80	5	97	5	90	4	45	11	75	2		15	34	57	93

Source: Macheath, J A (1982)

83

Chapter Seven

HOBBIES AND PASTIMES

Hobbies and pastimes include many and varied activities which can be pursued both inside and outside the home; alone or with others; costing very little or a fortune to participate; requiring very special equipment or clothing or just whatever one happens to have on at the time; requiring great physical prowess or little skill; expending a great deal of energy or almost no energy; by both men and women or just men or just women; by the young and/or the elderly.

Previous descriptive studies (e.g. Shanas et al 1968; Age Concern 1974 and 1977; Szalai, 1972; David, 1979 and Abrams, 1979, 1980) considered a variety of activities engaged in to varying degrees by the elderly. The following activities have been selected from these studies for consideration in this investigation, they being the activities to be found in at least two of the seven studies listed:-

listening to the radio	knitting
watching the television	sewing
reading the newspapers	crochet
reading books	gardening
reading magazines	playing cards

In order to participate in these activities varying degrees of mobility, skill and physical fitness are required. It must also be remembered that all the activities discussed may be pursued with equally varying levels of enthusiasm, vigour and depth. Many hobbies and pastimes are developed early in life and are then pursued into and throughout old age, whilst others may be developed later in life. There is a relationship between participation in an activity at various ages and the understanding of activities undertaken by the elderly. The level of this understanding is related to contact with the elderly in a variety of different roles in the Health and Social Services, whilst the image the elderly have of the activities of their peers differs considerably from those of the Health and Social Services staff.

1. Listening to the radio

Listening to the radio requires little physical effort and once the set is tuned almost no manual dexterity. However, a degree of hearing is a prerequisite for the enjoyment of this pastime regardless of the type of programme being listened to. This may well prove too big a barrier for a small number of the elderly, or indeed individuals of all ages. (Figure 7.1).

There is a gradual decline in the listening habits from the younger age group through to the mid-forties followed by a pronounced decrease in the forty five to fifty years age group. However, throughout old age, over 90.0% listen to the radio daily. This high proportion of the elderly listening to the radio may reflect lifetime habits developed through their experience of two world wars when news broadcasts were regularly listened to throughout the day together with the absence of television in their earlier years. The habits of the younger age groups may well reflect the availability of cheap portable radios today and the provision of car radios.

When those working with the elderly in a variety of situations are considered, their daily habits regarding radio listening are diverse and vary considerably from the habits of the elderly outlined above, many of whom are their patients (Figure 7.2).

As Figure 7.2 clearly illustrates few SRNs or SENs listen to the radio at all whereas all the Physical Educationalists listen regularly. Again too, fewer hospital-oriented staff than community-related staff listen to the radio regularly. No information is available as to the types of programmes followed nor the general time of day when listening predominates. It may well be that not only are the listening habits of the elderly and the younger staff of the Health, Education and Social Services very different but the actual programmes and the time of listening might also be very different. The listening habits of the more community related staff compare very favourably with those of the elderly themselves (see Figures 7.1 and 7.2).

The question may be raised whether the

particular occupation shapes the listening habits or whether individuals with particular lifestyles enter the various professions. It is interesting to note that a similar image is reflected when the understanding of the radio listening habits to the elderly are considered by profession. Only amongst the SRNs and Occupational Therapists do more than 50.0% believe that the elderly regularly listen to the radio, whilst less than 30.0% of the Aides believe their elderly patients listen to the radio. One must also wonder why only 66.0% of the Age Concern staff who work very closely with the elderly in the community believe elderly listen to radio programmes regularly.

The understanding of the radio listening habits of the elderly by the various age groups follow similar trends to the actual listening habits by age (Figure 7.1; Figure 7.3).

Apart from the 35-39 years and 45-49 years age groups, it is apparent that those who listen to the radio regularly themselves also believe that others do so. It suggests too, that contact with the elderly in the community increases the understanding of the radio listening habits of the elderly whilst those nursing the sick and infirm have little understanding of the listening habits of the elderly generally. Only 10.0% of the 45-49 years age group regularly tune into the radio but 40.0% believe the elderly do so. This may reflect observation of their elderly parents in the war years rather than currently. Over the age of sixty five years almost everyone believes their peers listen to the radio daily.

Obviously the younger age groups all believe the elderly sit and watch television every day (see Figure 7.3). Viewing television requires one to be virtually inactive and sitting before the set. Radio listening can take place as one goes about other tasks. The elderly appear to believe they are on the go doing things around the house (see Chapters 4-6) and could listen to the radio as they go about these tasks. However, the elderly could not be as busy as they intimate if their television habits were as the younger staff believe.

The listening habits of the elderly of the 1980s compare favourably with those of their peers in the 1960s as illustrated by the Shanas et al (1968) study. 63% of those aged 65-69 years living alone in that study listened to the radio on the day prior to being interviewed. These individuals would be in the over 80 age group in the 1980s study outlined above in which over 90% of all elderly regularly listen to the radio. However, Abrams (1980) suggests that a 'substantial majority' (40%) of his sample do not normally listen to the radio, but 66% of his over 75 years age group felt that there had been no change in their listening habits. Do these diverse studies suggest that the elderly vary in their radio listening habits in different parts of the country or is it just that the groups investigated are as equally diverse, or is it that the age groups are considerably larger in the Abrams (1980) and Shanas et al (1968) studies (these being just over 75 years, and the Macheath (1982) study being 75-79 years and over 80 years)? It must also be remembered that those aged over 75 years in the Shanas et al (1968) study would be at least over 88 years in the Abrams (1980) and Macheath (1982) studies. This is not the case though when the two latter studies are considered. Even the over 80 years age group may span twenty years and perhaps should be further broken down for many of this age group would have been ardent crystal set users in their youth before the wireless became an everyday item.

2. **Watching Television**
Watching televison has been an integral part of family life for the past twenty years. However, those aged over sixty five years (i.e. the elderly) have had the greater part of their lives without television being readily accessible or available to them as a means of news bulletins and entertainment. One would expect these factors together with the high incidence of listening to the radio in old age to, perhaps, be reflected in the viewing habits of the older age groups. On the contrary, though, one can still enjoy viewing television even as one's hearing deteriorates especially with the development of sub titles and other aids for these individuals in recent years.

When considering television, notice must also be taken of the channel preferences and the wide variety of programmes offered for these will reflect the background, interests, tastes and lifestyles of the different age groups. Will the same correlation between self participation and the understanding of elderly participation highlighted in radio listening be apparent in relation to television viewing? Are the viewing habits similar in the different age groups? (Figure 7.4).

Figure 7.4 clearly illustrates that almost all those aged between thirty and sixty years of age watch television daily, but from sixty to eighty years of age only 70.0% view daily and over eighty years of age there is a further drop to 60.0% who view television daily. This is the reverse pattern to daily radio listening (see Figure 7.1).

From the available data it is apparent that the elderly watch BBC1 throughout old age to a high degree but relatively few watch ITV. In contrast, those below retirement age (i.e. the staff) tend to watch more ITV but rarely view BBC2 (see Figure 7.5).

With such variations between the age groups in their channel viewing preferences it may well be that a similar pattern emerges in the actual types of programmes viewed by the different age groups. A range of programmes will be considered without reference to specific channels in order to establish whether or not differing viewing patterns do in fact exist between the under sixty years of age groups (i.e. the staff) and the elderly. Some general trends emerge regarding the viewing of the news; quiz programmes; serials; sports programmes; documentaries; films; wildlife programmes; and children's programmes.

The variations in possible programme viewing may be related to channel preference, but further investigation is necessary prior to establishing such a correlation.

Table 7.1 illustrates considerable viewing differences between the two staff groups (A and B) themselves, between the two elderly groups (C and D) and between the staff (A and B) and the elderly (C and D). Wildlife and films are the two types of programme showing the greatest fluctuations with age. Quiz programmes generally hold little appeal for any of the four groups. However the reverse is true of the children's programmes. Few staff readily admit to seeing these programmes - maybe because of work or family commitments - but they are popular with the over eighty year olds, being second only to the news, which follows the major childrens presentation each day. The timing of particular programmes in relation to viewing habits may also be worthy of consideration, for example, do the elderly not watch films because many are shown late in the day?

Although both the young and the very old view the news to a high level, almost all of the under forty year olds but only 78.0% of the over eighty year olds view the news on television. Figures 7.6 and 7.7 indicate the viewing levels of the staff in the seven age groups up to sixty years of age in comparison to those of their elderly patients in the five age groups over the age of sixty years, breaking down the more general classifications in Table 7.1 . Most of the categories could be further investigated in relation to channel selection and the actual types of particular programmes viewed, for example, serials can mean 'Coronation Street', Dickens books in serial form; Le Carre novels in serial form; and a quiz can be Mastermind; Ask the Family; panel games; a Question of Sport, etc. Just as there are considerable differences between the staff of Health, Education, and Social Services and their elderly patients outlined in Figure 7.6 and 7.7 there are likely to be variations of viewing habits and selections within most of the general categories.

Whereas relatively few of those in the younger age groups believed that the elderly listened to the radio regularly, a very high percentage believed that the elderly regularly view television (see Figure 7.2). This appears to parallel their own viewing habits. However this is not the case with those over the age of sixty years for more believe their peers watch television regularly than actually view it themselves. It appears that the staff believe that watching television is a major activity of their elderly patients. It would be interesting to investigate the actual types of programmes they believe the elderly watch and which channels they believe the elderly predominantly select.

When staff qualifications are considered, there are not only wide differences between the various professional groups but also between their understanding of the viewing habits of their elderly patients and clients. (Table 7.2).

Almost all the staff working with the elderly believe that their elderly clients regularly watch television whereas less than 50.0% believe they listen to the radio. This is a very different image to the actual viewing habits of the elderly themselves outlined above. When channel selection, programme choice, and viewing habits are considered together the discrepancy between the staff and their patients/clients widens further. Many of the staff see television as an ideal activity - or non activity is probably better - for the elderly whether they wish to watch it or not. Many elderly individuals sitting before a television set often are not viewing but sleeping, or just relaxing. In many rooms the television has replaced the hearth as the focal point for furniture arrangement. Television also stunts the social skills of yesteryear for many elderly individuals. Watching television excludes conversation and the leisure time pursuits of reading, sewing, knitting, etc that demand use of the eyes elsewhere, whereas these activities could occur as one listened to the radio.

Age Concern (1977) suggests that 91% of those aged over sixty five years of age watch television at least one hour each day, but the Age Concern (1974) study suggests that only 25% actually enjoyed this experience. The National Council on Aging (1974) study of Americans, also using the all embracing ageing, indicates that 93% of their sample watch television generally but only 82% watch at least one hour each day. In contrast, only 45% of those aged 65-69 and 41% of those aged 70-74 in the Shanas et al (1968) investigation watched television. At the time of this study it must be remembered that owning a television set was still considered a relatively expensive luxury item for many people. The results of this Shanas et al (1968) investigation compare closely with the data outlined above in Figures 7.4 - 7.7 of the Macheath (1982) age related study. However ownership of a television set in the 1980s appears to be almost universal according to Abrams (1980). In the 65-74 age group 44% owned a coloured television set and 56% owned a black and white set, whilst in the over 75 age group the figures were 30% and 66% respectively. These figures suggest that only approximately 4% of those elderly living in the community do not actually own a television set.

Abrams (1980) indicates that those aged over 75 years spend longer watching television than listening to the radio and 33% of this age group felt that they had increased the amount of time they watched television over the past four years. This may be for many reasons and is in need of further detailed consideration. None of these past studies addressed themselves to the channels viewed or the specific programmes selected by the various age groups, thus consideration of the changes in recent years is unfortunately not possible at this stage.

It is apparent that the television viewing habits of the current generations of elderly men and women are determined by attitudes and habits formed in their earlier years. These independent individuals do not view television for hours on end for they have other hobbies and pursuits and routines that do not include viewing for the sake of it. However, future generations of elderly who have viewed endless television throughout their earlier habit forming years may well be very different as they progress into and through old age in the decades ahead.

3. **Reading**
One might expect less physically active people to
enjoy the more sedentary leisuretime pursuits.
However, reading papers, books, and magazines
presupposes adequate eyesight and a reasonable level
of reading ability. Reading for the elderly has been
enhanced in recent years with the advent of large
print books, but it must be remembered that
newspapers and magazines do not usually provide this
facility apart from the headlines.
Material for reading comes from many sources for
the elderly and may or may not involve cost. Mobile
libraries in the rural areas have increased the
access to books for many individuals who otherwise
would be unable to borrow books regularly. Newspapers
are part of the daily routine for many elderly as
they keep abreast of national events and their own
particular interests. However, the increasing cost
of the daily paper may have an adverse effect in the
near future on the elderly in this respect. (Table
7.3).

Newspapers. Macheath (1982) in Table 7.3 shows that
daily newspaper reading is an activity for all age
groups, but in retirement almost everyone under
eighty years of age makes it part of their daily
routine as do 80% of the very old. Age Concern (1977)
supports this high level of newspaper reading by the
elderly (91.0%) but the Hunt (1978) study suggests
that only 74.0% of those aged over sixty five years
read newspapers. Americans do not read as much as
their British peers according to Robinson (1977) who
says only 18.0% of those aged over fifty five years
read newspapers.
Reading the newspapers can mean everything from
taking in every word, to looking at the pictures
only, to just reading the headlines, to reading only
particular parts of the newspaper. Indeed it is known
that some individuals who cannot read take a daily
newspaper and look at the pictures in order not to
admit they cannot read. Thus, each elderly individual
will have her own approach to this activity and
indeed her own preference for a particular newspaper
for a variety of reasons. Usually elderly individuals
still read the newspaper they had in their earlier
years, that they know their way around very well.
Prior to the television and radio reporting of events
today, the newspaper was, perhaps, the only means for
one to learn what was happening elsewhere and to read
of events that had occurred weeks or months

previously, especially at times of crisis (e.g. 1914-1918 war). These habits of earlier years are well founded and apparent in the current generations of elderly people regarding reading of newspapers.

Books. Fewer elderly people read books than read newspapers, but even so, more elderly read books (49.0%) than the younger members of society and this does not decrease with age (Macheath 1982). Hunt (1978) supports this view of elderly book reading habits (53.0%) but Age Concern (1977) gave a much lower involvement figure (39.0%). Very few older Americans read books (5.5%) (Robinson 1977) whilst Hunt (1978) found that more women than men (5.1%:40.6%) read books throughout old age.

Only 26.0. of the Health, Education, and Social Services staff making up the under 60 years age group read books regularly, whereas almost 50.0% of their elderly parents read books regularly. It would be interesting, too, to compare the types of books that appeal to these two sectors of the community alongside the sources of such materials. Reading is a stimulating activity for the elderly with books readily accessible today. Indeed selecting a book to read is a stimulating experience in itself and if a trip to the library is involved, socialising and leaving the home are also important. Miller (1963) suggested that many elderly individuals used passed on spectacles which did not necessarily suit their needs. This affected their use of books. Today, though, big print books allow the elderly to read easily and enjoyably provided they can support the added weight of the book comfortably.

Magazines. Many elderly individuals read magazines that are passed on to them by friends and relations rather than purchasing them themselves. Reading magazines, therefore, may depend on others and access to them. The print in magazines is often more difficult for those with defective vision or poor lighting which could have ramifications for the elderly who are renowned for not getting their eyes tested or putting on extra lights.

A few more elderly Americans read magazines (8.0%:5.5%) than read books, but this is not the image of the British elderly. Fewer men than women read magazines (33.0%:51.8%) (Hunt 1978), but this may be because women's magazines are of a more general nature and are more readily accessible. The

Macheath (1982) data in Table 7.3 does not support
the high Hunt (1978) level of magazine reading by the
elderly (7.0%). Very few of the younger elderly read
magazines and only 12.0% of the older elderly do so.
If cost was a factor, one might expect the reverse to
be the case. Overall, only a small minority of the
over sixty year olds appear to read any magazines
regularly, but almost as many staff read magazines as
read books regularly (see Table 7.3).

Comments. 1.0% of the elderly gave up reading (Age
Concern 1974) whilst 22.0% would like to read more
books and 17.0% more newspapers and magazines (Age
Concern 1977). 17.8% are said NOT to read and only
7.1% say they actually enjoy reading (Hunt 1978) with
only 3.0% looking forward to reading (Age Concern
1974). When time given to reading is considered 1.3
hours were spent reading on the day prior to the
Abrams (1980) interviews by elderly individuals.
    48.9% of the Americans believe that their
elderly population read a little (National Council on
Aging 1974). The British believe their elderly read
to a much greater extent, but the younger members of
society have lower belief levels than do the elderly
as Table 7.3 clearly indicates (Macheath 1982). The
levels of beliefs increase throughout old age which
may be associated with a parallel decrease in
personal mobility and physical activity. When the
staff beliefs regarding television and reading are
considered together, it is apparent that the non-
physical pursuits are seen to be suitable and
expected activities of the elderly by the staff
working with them in the process of rehabilitation to
the exclusion of more physical pursuits. One must
wonder if these attitudes are instilled in the basic
training courses of the professions concerned or if
they are acquired in the practical situation.

4. **Cards**
Card playing, along with bingo, are generally
believed to be activities of elderly people and a
major activity in Clubs for the elderly. Data that is
available, though, does not readily support such a
hypothesis totally. 13.0% of elderly people play
cards two or three times each month and the same
number would like to play more (Age Concern 1977). In
more recent data (Macheath 1982), much higher
participation levels are indicated - 62.2% (65-69
years); 64.5% (70-74 years); 65.8% (75-79 years) and

54.7% (over 80 years) which tend to support the general belief that card playing, in whatever form, is an elderly leisuretime pursuit in many areas of the country. A high proportion of the staff of all ages believe the elderly play cards regularly, although more older staff than younger staff believe this to be the case.

```
Under 30 years   -   55.0%
30 - 39 years    -   43.0%
40 - 49 years    -   55.0%
50 - 59 years    -   84.0%
```

In contrast, almost all the elderly of all ages believe their peers are regular card players:-

```
60 - 70 years    -   87.0%
70 - 80 years    -  100.0%
Over 80 years    -   97.0%
```

illustrating that the belief that their peers play cards is considerably higher than their own actual participation levels. Card playing can be a stimulating, social activity involving manual dexterity. For many of the less mobile, and indeed their more mobile peers, it gives an opportunity to not only play at Clubs, but also at locally arranged Whist Drives, etc.

It must be remembered, too, that card playing can also take place in the home. Here it may be a cross generation activity where everyone can compete on equal terms or it may be a solitary pursuit. Card games such as bridge or poker are again governed by different codes and mores according to when and where they are being played, but they are played by people of all ages into and throughout old age. No evidence is available as to the types of card games enjoyed by the elderly.

5. Knitting and Sewing

Knitting and sewing, although two activities often thought of together, require totally different basic skills to make participation possible. Sewing involves finer manipulative skills and better eyesight than knitting. This may be reflected in the participation habits of the elderly. Those with bad arthritic hands, which may slow down their knitting, will be very much greater impeded when sewing or trying to thread the needle to sew. In general terms,

one either knits or sews, participating occasionally
in the other activity. Both these activities are
basically female pursuits.
    29.0% of all elderly aged over sixty years knit
and 22.0% would be interested in knitting more (Age
Concern 1977). This figure compares favourably with
the earlier Age Concern (1974) data when 20.8%
reported knitting and 12.2% sewed. 0.5% of the men
reported knitting but none admitted to sewing in this
earlier study.
    Macheath (1982) reported many more elderly
knitting or sewing regularly into and throughout old
age. Twice as many elderly knit as sew perhaps
supporting the hypothesis that the finer skills are
required for the latter which are lost in old age.
Older people knit and sew more than the under forty
year olds in the Health, Education, and Social
Services who work with them. Many more of the staff
believe their elderly patients knit than sew but
their belief levels nowhere match those of the
elderly themselves whose belief levels often
overmatch their actual participation levels
(Macheath 1982). (See Table 7.4).
    Many older people knitted for the war effort in
their earlier years and now knit for their children
and grandchildren. The older generations viewed
sewing as a necessity for making clothes last that
little bit longer during the wars and depression or
adjusting them for other members of the family,
whereas the younger staff have been raised on manmade
fibres and fast changing fashions. These social
habits may well reflect the current attitudes of the
different age groups regarding sewing either as a
creative hobby or to "make do and mend". These two
pursuits still play a major role in the keeping
busy/doing something lifestyles of the elderly
today. Many Clubs for the elderly use oddments of
wool etc. to make squares for blankets as do the
hospitalised elderly through occupational therapy,
which are then sewn or crocheted together for use.
Good eyesight is not a pre-requisite for such an
activity. (Table 7.4).
    There is a considerable decrease in the knitting
habits of the elderly in their seventies which picks
up again in the over eighty year olds, but this is
not the case with sewing. Knitting is one of the few
activities that both the staff over the age of thirty
five years and their elderly patients pursue at
similar levels, although the actual styles and wools
used and items produced may be very different. At
least this is one area of activity where

communication could readily occur in the course of rehabilitation contact.

6. Crochet and Embroidery

Only a small number of any age crochet or embroider. Again it is the older individuals who follow these pursuits occasionally. There is a marked increase in interest over the age of sixty five years, but shows a considerable decline throughout old age regarding embroidery. This steady decline may not be the result of declining interest but deterioriation of vision and/or manual dexterity.

Just 9.0% of those crocheting and 27.0% who admit they embroider were aged under sixty five years. 54.0% crochet and 29.3% embroider into and throughout old age (Macheath 1982). More older elderly (over 80 years) crochet than younger elderly which possibly reflects the ease of the skill involved in relation to eyesight and the manual dexterity required for success. Fewer elderly crochet though than knit or even sew.

Many of these skills are used occasionally when Clubs or Groups knit or crochet squares for blankets. These are often made, too, as part of therapy in hospitals and Day Hospitals or Centres under the aegis of the occupational therapist. The cost of wool is often a factor that prevents elderly knitting or crocheting for their families as gifts but blankets are made from oddments donated by the community.

7. Gardening

Gardening can mean anything from pottering amongst the roses or flower borders to digging a large vegetable patch and hand mowing large lawns. The former requires little strength or stamina whilst the latter certainly demands a reasonable fitness level. How an individual perceives gardening in relation to her current situation will determine the level of involvement.

Many elderly people have moved from large family homes to small bungalows or apartments and thus lose their gardens very often. Other elderly men undertake allotments on retirement and increase their gardening activities which may have then to be curtailed by disability or declining years later. More men than women have difficulty with gardening through disability (5.3%:1.2%) (Hunt 1978). This may reflect the types of gardening undertaken by the different sexes for men usually see the heavy work as their contribution whilst women take on the lighter aspects of gardening. 47.1% were unable to do heavy gardening work and 19.3% lighter aspects of gardening for a variety of reasons (Hunt 1978). Hunt (1978) suggests that 23.1% of elderly living alone are well able to garden easily whilst a further 21.1% garden with some difficulty, but another 21.1% have no garden in which to work.

8.0% of all elderly had given up gardening and 58.0% either did the garden themselves or their spouse did it (Age Concern 1974). Hunt (1978) and Macheath (1982) support the high level of regular gardening activities though Macheath (1982) demonstrates that involvement declines with age – 58.3% (65-69 years); 33.3% (70-74 years); 41.4% (75-79 years) and 11.3% (over 80 years). The sudden decrease in participation in the over eighties may be the result of a change in living arrangements by the very old. In contrast, few of the younger staff working with the elderly garden regularly – 13.6% (35-39 years); 7.6% (30-34 years) and 15.1% (under 29 years). Americans have the reverse trend where older women spend 12 minutes per day gardening whilst the times for the younger American women are under 30 years – 2 minutes; 30-39 years – 2 minutes; 40-45 years – 3 minutes and 46-54 years – 2 minutes. The corresponding times for the American men are 1,1,3,1 and 2 respectively (Robinson 1977). It appears that pottering in the garden in the United States, if done at all, is done by the older women and this possibly indicates that very little actual gardening takes place.

Americans believe that older people do indeed garden a little (47.3%) and even a lot (36.0%). More British also believe that the elderly garden regularly. Almost all age groups of staff have such belief levels above 50.0% - only the 35-39 years age groups drops to 32.0%. Over 97.0% of the elderly believe that their peers garden regularly. It must be remembered though, that no indication of what gardening actually involves is available. Gardening is relaxing and therapeutic. It can be done outside, in a greenhouse, or even inside with houseplants and window boxes, and as such could be available and a valuable aid to rehabilitation for all elderly of all ages. Even tending the houseplants can be time consuming, therapeutic, and involve a modicum of physical activity without actually going outside the home. Elderly people of all ages enjoy receiving plants from friends and relations, many of which can be planted out afterwards. These activities, if recognised by the staff work endeavour to rehabilitate and/or maintain the elderly in the community can be well used as motivations in the early stages. Gardening may involve producing vegetables, growing flowers, or both. It is the latter that most elderly people consider appropriate, even in the towns and cities. Even the smallest gardens can be very productive. However, it is the getting down to ground level and up again that often presents problems for the elderly be it for seed planting, weeding, or harvesting the crops. Many whose arthritis prevents them getting down bend from the waist which can then lead to other problems. Given normal conditions gardening is an ideal activity for the elderly men and women which can be pursued despite considerable health problems throughout old age for one can be busy moving and doing for many hours using the hands, bending and stretching, twisting and turning, fetching and carrying, watering and weeding, provided it is adapted to each individual's capabilities.

SUMMARY

The current generations of elderly have been brought up in their earlier years to keep busy, to make things that they required, to do things for themselves, to mend clothes, replace buttons, and darn holes, etc. and be self-sufficient. These traits are now apparent in their hobbies and pastimes in later life. The elderly today do read, listen to the radio, watch a little television, knit, sew, and garden as regular parts of their disciplined lives. It is a pity that the younger professional staff in the Health, Education, and Social Services who work with the elderly in the rehabilitative process fail to see them in this light and do not believe activities and hobbies are in fact part of old age. The only activity that these younger staff believe the elderly do to any great extent is watch television. This may be so whilst they are in the hospital surroundings, for it is available and put on for them, but in the community their lives appear to be centred around many other hobbies and pastimes. The current generation of elderly people appears to be much more involved in leisure time activities than their children or grandchildren who have had man-made amusements for most or all of their lives. The elderly today, in their formative years, would have been busy doing things with their hands whilst listening to the wireless and this has been the way with them into and throughout old age.

Unless the up and coming generations of elderly are weened away from television towards more constructive leisure time pursuits, they will have many problems to face and come to terms with as they progress into and through to old age. With improved health in earlier years and earlier retirement they should be better equipped to fulfil long, busy, and productive later lives than the current generations of elderly people who have survived major health hazards, wars, poverty, shortages of food, etc. in order to be elderly today.

If the staff of the Health, Education, and Social Services see the elderly as a group who should be pursuing non-active hobbies and pastimes (e.g. television) and do not believe they are indeed busy and participating in active pursuits it may be a problem for those responsible for the rehabilitation of the elderly in changing these attitudes. Communication of positive attitudes, positive encouragement, and positive ideas are an important part of the process especially in the early stages of rehabilitation. It is also important that all the professions concerned with not only the rehabilitation of the elderly but also the maintenance of their independence and freedom in the community appreciate the importance of many of the hobbies and pastimes in this process and in the past and present lives of their elderly patients/clients, for only then will these members of the caring Health, Education, and Social Services be able to offer advice and encouragement that is appropriate and comprehended.

FIGURE 7.1

Listening Daily to the Radio by Age

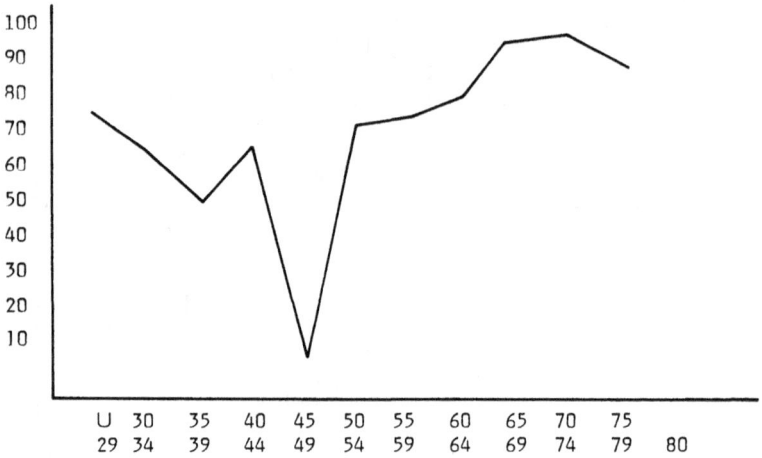

| | U 29 | 30 34 | 35 39 | 40 44 | 45 49 | 50 54 | 55 59 | 60 64 | 65 69 | 70 74 | 75 79 | 80 |

FIGURE 7.2

Regular Listening to the Radio and Beliefs Regarding Elderly Listening Habits by Profession

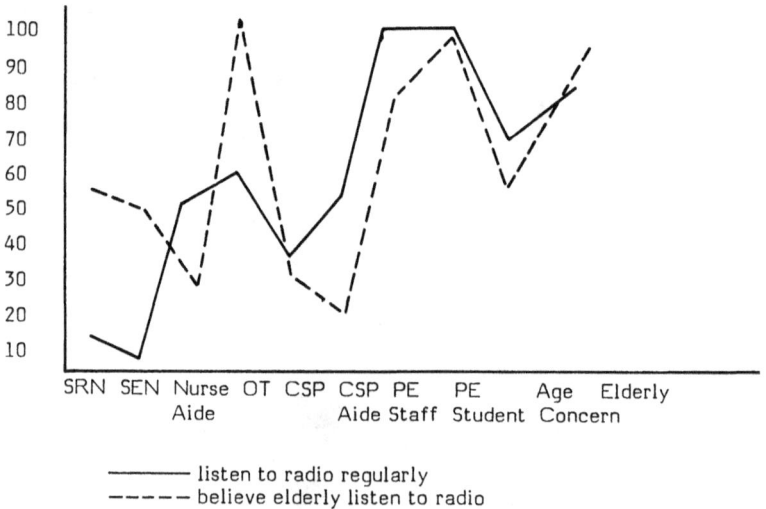

SRN SEN Nurse OT CSP CSP PE PE Age Elderly
Aide Aide Staff Student Concern

——————— listen to radio regularly
— — — — believe elderly listen to radio

FIGURE 7.3

The Understanding of the Radio Listening and
Television Viewing Daily Habits of the Elderly by Age

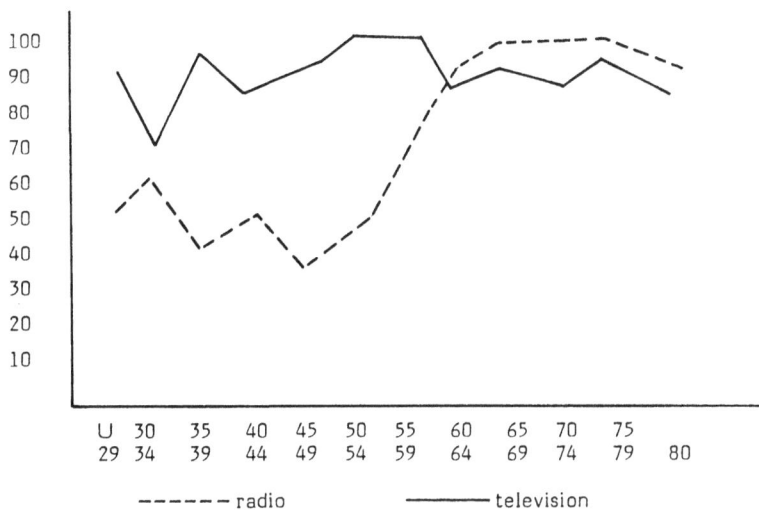

| | U
29 | 30
34 | 35
39 | 40
44 | 45
49 | 50
54 | 55
59 | 60
64 | 65
69 | 70
74 | 75
79 | 80 |

------- radio   ———— television

FIGURE 7.4

Television Viewing Daily by Age

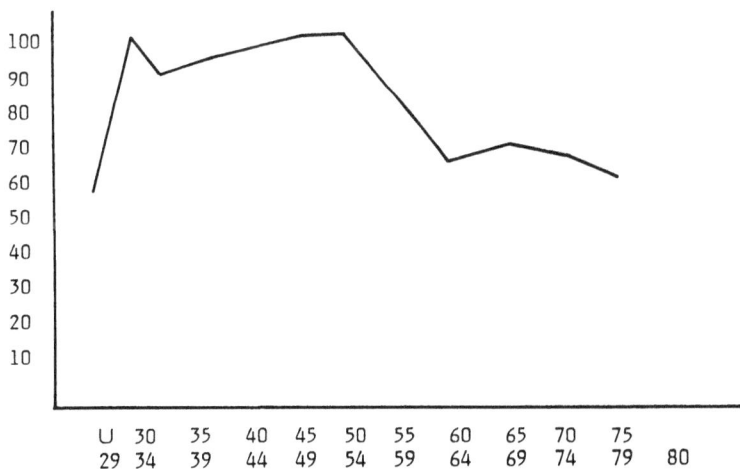

| | U
29 | 30
34 | 35
39 | 40
44 | 45
49 | 50
54 | 55
59 | 60
64 | 65
69 | 70
74 | 75
79 | 80 |

FIGURE 7.5

Television Channels Viewed Regularly by Age

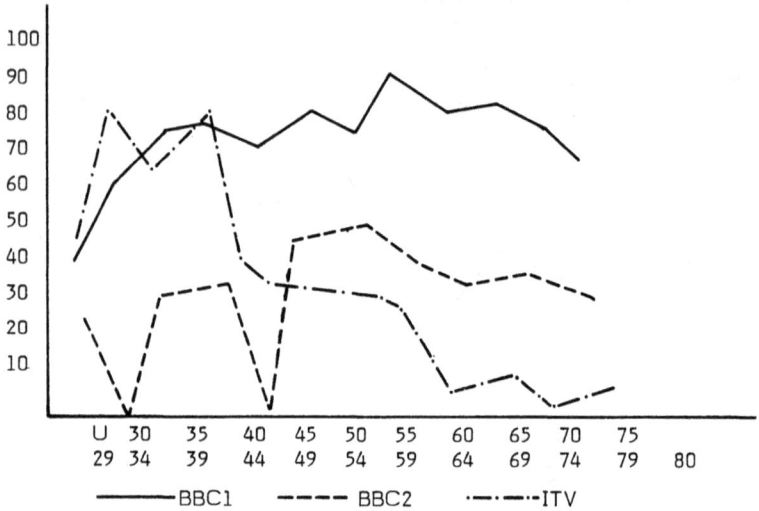

| | U 29 | 30 34 | 35 39 | 40 44 | 45 49 | 50 54 | 55 59 | 60 64 | 65 69 | 70 74 | 75 79 | 80 |

─────── BBC1   ─ ─ ─ BBC2   ─·─·─ ITV

FIGURE 7.6

Viewing of Selected Television Programmes by Age

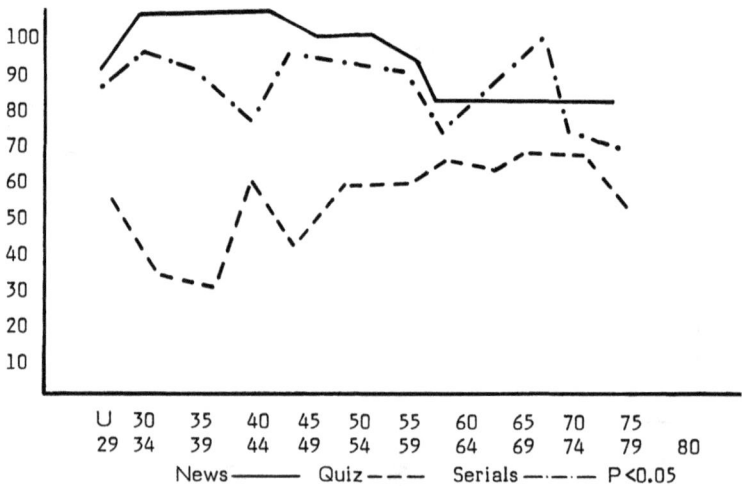

| | U 29 | 30 34 | 35 39 | 40 44 | 45 49 | 50 54 | 55 59 | 60 64 | 65 69 | 70 74 | 75 79 | 80 |

News ───────   Quiz ─ ─ ─   Serials ─·─·─   P <0.05

102

FIGURE 7.7

Viewing Selected Television Programmes by Age

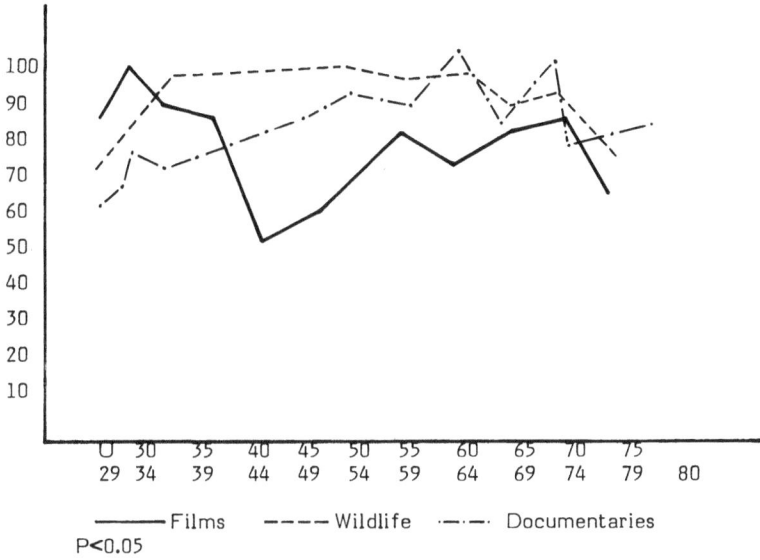

| | 30 | 35 | 40 | 45 | 50 | 55 | 60 | 65 | 70 | 75 | |
| 29 | 34 | 39 | 44 | 49 | 54 | 59 | 64 | 69 | 74 | 79 | 80 |

————Films   ————Wildlife   ·—·— Documentaries

P<0.05

103

TABLE 7.1

A Comparative Order of Programme Viewing by Age

Rank	A Under 29	B 40-49	C 60-79	D Over 80
1.	News	Documentary	Wildlife	News
2.	Films	Wildlife	Documentary	Children
3.	Serials	News	News	Documentary
4.	Wildlife	Serial	Film	Wildlife
5.	Documentary	Sport	Children	Serials
6.	Sport	Film	Serial	Film
7.	Quiz	Quiz	Quiz	Sport
8.	Children	Children	Sport	Quiz

Source: Macheath, J A (1982)

TABLE 7.2

Qualifications, Viewing Habits, and Understanding of Elderly Viewing Habits

	% View television regularly	% believe elderly view television regularly
S.R.N.	35	85
S. E.N.	80	95
Nurse Aide	85	95
Occupational Therapist	100	100
Physiotherapist	100	100
O.T./C.S.P Aide	80	100
P.E. Staff	100	100
Students	100	100
Age Concern Staff	90	100
Elderly Club Staff	95	95

Source: Macheath, J A (1982)

TABLE 7.3

% Reading Daily and % Believing that
Elderly Read Regularly by Age

| | Read Daily | | | Believe Elderly |
	Papers	Books	Magazines	Read Regularly
Under 29	54	24	12	75
30-34 years	76	28	30	58
35-39 years	76	20	20	30
40-44 years	82	30	30	52
44-49 years	66	15	0	68
50-54 years	72	33	28	40
55-59 years	82	28	0	72
60-64 years	100	38	12	72
65-69 years	100	58	0	65
70-74 years	96	48	8	95
75-79 years	100	52	4	100
Over 80 years	80	50	12	90

Source: Macheath, J A (1982)

TABLE 7.4

% Knitting and Sewing Regularly and
% Believing the Elderly Knit and Sew Regularly by Age

	Knit	Sew	Believe Elderly Knit	Sew
	Regularly		Regularly	
Under 29 years	21.2	15.1	52	33
30-34 years	7.6	0.0	2.4	15
36-39 years	40.9	18.1	64	18
40-44 years	41.6	29.1	50	33
45-49 years	50.0	37.3	50	33
50-54 years	54.5	45.4	65	36
55-59 years	54.5	36.3	52	45
60-64 years	75.0	37.5	100	62
65-69 years	50.0	29.1	95	97
70-74 years	31.2	22.9	97	95
75-79 years	46.3	34.2	90	85
Over 80 years	52.8	24.5	92	75

Source: Macheath, J A (1982)

Chapter Eight

ATTITUDES TO ASPECTS OF EXERCISE

The beliefs and attitudes of the elderly and the staff of the Health, Education, and Social Services assisting them in the rehabilitative process have a bearing on how they perceive exercise not only in terms of their own lives but also the lives of other people. These beliefs and attitudes will be reflected in their fears and desires regarding participation in regular physical activities. Past experiences, good or bad, will also play a major part in the formation of any such beliefs and attitudes. Should the beliefs and attitudes be too diverse, problems of communication and understanding may ensue between the elderly and those staff involved in their rehabilitation as a result of inappropriate advice being offered.

Consideration must be given to some specific questions regarding the attitudes to exercise of the elderly and the groups of staff with whom they may become involved, namely:-

(a) How do these two groups actually perceive exercise?

(b) How do they view talking to others about exercise?

(c) How do they all view elderly men and women who actually participate in various forms of physical activities?

(d) What are their fears regarding actual participation in physical activities and what would make such an experience an enjoyable one rather than a penance?

PERCEPTIONS OF EXERCISE

The meaning of the term exercise varies from one individual to another. It will also vary at different stages of life and will reflect one's interests in the more physical pursuits at any given time. Such a definition might also change with age and fitness levels.

Macheath (1982) reports that the elderly view exercise as a more positive aspect of their lives than the staff in the Health, Education, and Social Services working with them. As Table 8.1 illustrates, 10.0% of the elderly, but 20.0% of the staff view exercise negatively. 31.0% of the elderly state that it is what is needed and wanted but just 9.0% of the staff shared this positive approach to exercise. (Table 8.1).

When the 'what is wanted and needed' is expanded to include that it is 'important, necessary, good, right, and what should be done' the position overall illustrates the differences between staff in these caring and providing services and the elderly with whom they work are considerable (62.0%:82.0%). It is surprising that more staff in these rehabilitative services do not see exercise as important or necessary (14.0%) when such aspects should be the core of their work on the road to getting their elderly patients back on their feet in the community.

These responses support the earlier Macheath (1978) study of elderly attitudes to exercise when comments such as:- "Its the person's age, and the state of their health for instance ... we don't know how far we can go strenuously, each of us is different" and "It helps pull you together, you've got to keep going, haven't you" "Its the whole object of the thing isn't it, to get you out and about, and movement, isn't it" were reported.

With so many staff not seeing exercise as necessary one must wonder what attitudes they in fact pass on to their patients and how these attitudes have been acquired. Are they acquired through what is included or excluded in the basic training programmes or do they result from the attitudes of others in the working situation?

TALKING TO OTHERS ABOUT EXERCISE

This aspect of exercise and the attitudes to it are crucial if changes are to take place, beliefs be exchanged, and attitudes modified. Communication will only occur if both parties involved comprehend exercise in similar terms and are willing to share their beliefs and attitudes with each other. Staff involved in talking to patients about the importance of physical activity in the rehabilitation process must also appreciate the differences in comprehension held by those with whom they are endeavouring to advise. Both parties must see talking about exercise as both necessary and important at that particular moment in time.

Macheath (1982) reported vast discrepancies between the elderly and the groups of staff when positive attitudes to the talking about exercise to others were investigated. 66.0% of the elderly felt that more discussion about exercise would be a good idea whilst 39.0% felt it to be necessary, important, or helpful. Only 2.0% of the elderly regarded this as an unimportant activity and 5.0% saw it as an activity to be undertaken only by "those who know or it was part of their job specifically". Thus almost one third of the staff working with the elderly in a variety of situations are reported as having negative approaches to the talking to others about exercise. Only 21.0% of the staff felt that more discussion would be a good idea; 8.0% felt it necessary, important, and helpful. No staff felt that it would be really helpful to talk in any way quite regardless of whom they were talking to. With only 29.0% of the staff holding relatively positive views on talking to others about exercise and over one third with very definitely negative views on such an activity, further investigation is urgently required to consider the effect this might be having on the rehabilitation of the elderly through the advice being offered and the encouragement, or lack of it, being given. These responses illustrate the great diversity of beliefs and attitudes between the staff in the Health, Education, and Social Services and the elderly with whom they work. Both parties also have diverse beliefs regarding the needs of the elderly to know what they should do in the field of physical activity.

It is surprising that 2.0% of these rehabilitative staff do not see talking to the elderly about exercise as part of their job and another 14.0% consider it to be a waste of time or unimportant. One really must wonder what these staff consider they should be doing to rehabilitate the elderly into the activities of daily living which themselves are forms of exercise demanding a degree of fitness to perform.

Many elderly (66.0%) believe that talking about exercise, what they should or could do, is not done enough. This illustrates that they are not getting the advice they want and feel they need from the

Health, Education, and Social Service staff following illness or injury. The elderly apparently are looking for guidance, from staff who do not generally see this as an important, necessary, or helpful part of their role in the process of rehabilitation. If these staff are not undertaking such tasks positively to whom are the elderly to turn to apart from their peers. (Table 8.2).

ATTITUDES REGARDING ELDERLY MEN AND WOMEN WHO ACTUALLY PARTICIPATE IN PHYSICAL ACTIVITIES

It might be supposed that the attitudes and beliefs regarding elderly participation in various physical activities would follow the trends outlined above regarding perceptions of exercise (see Table 8.1) and the attitudes and beliefs regarding talking to others about exercise (see Table 8.2).

As Table 8.3 indicates, the results reported by Macheath (1982) fall into three general categories - the results of exercise for the elderly themselves; who the elderly are who participate in exercise; and a general group of rather negative characteristics. Once again this latter group consists of one third of the staff, with half that group actually believing that the elderly rarely exercise at all, but no elderly appear in this group. Thus a definite trend emerges.

The elderly have very positive attitudes regarding their peers who do participate in many forms of physical activity. Perhaps this is the result of their own observations of friends and/or relatives who do take part in some form of exercise. Despite 32.0% of the staff believing that elderly who exercise are better for it only an additional 12.0% have other positive attitudes. In contrast, 61.0% of the elderly believe that their peers are better for participating and in addition 63.0% also have other positive beliefs regarding their peers' particip- ation in physical pursuits (some indicated more than one response). Similar numbers of staff and elderly (25.0%:32.0%) see those elderly participating in many forms of exercise as the healthier, fitter, younger ones, but within these small groups there are indeed differences. For example, more staff see the fitter younger elderly participating while more elderly see their participating peers as having done such exercise all their lives and are therefore the healthier ones.

A similar percentage of elderly have positive

perceptions of exercise and positive beliefs regarding talking to others about exercise. Similar percentages of the staff believe exercise is good/right as believe elderly who exercise keep fitter and healthier, but the staffs:elderly ratio is 1:2 in these positive categories (Table 8.3).

16.0% of the staff believe that very few elderly in fact exercise, with a further 4.0% believing the elderly never do it, and 5.0% believing they should not do it. An overall 25.0% of the staff obviously do not see their elderly patients as participating in the very activities that will assist them in the maintenance of their independence and freedom in the community. This is in harmony with the earlier discussion (Chapter 7) highlighting the staff view that generally they believe all the elderly do is sit and watch television throughout their passing years. In contrast 30.0% of the elderly believe those who exercise do well and enjoy life.

The more positive attitudes outlined in Table 8.3 are well supported by the Macheath (1978) study of a small select group of elderly people in Ramsgate, Kent and Peasenhall, Suffolk. All were agreed that exercise led to a sense of well being and those who participate were better for it.

THE FEARS AND PLEASURES OF EXERCISE PARTICIPATION

The attitudes reflected above may well be influenced by the fears of people regarding any participation in physical activities and what they believe makes such an experience an enjoyable one. Any inherent fears may well prevent an individual from even contemplating taking up a new activity or returning to an activity after a lengthy break.

The main fears of the elderly are those of the younger population, namely getting tired or exhausted and getting injured or hurt followed by the fear of not being able to actually do the activity or pushing it too hard. These are well recognised fears of individuals coming into exercise programmes. The staff have these same fears but in addition fear of being forced to participate which may be related to compulsory participation in their schooldays.

The main fears of the elderly can readily be overcome by talking with them about exercise more which 66.0% of them felt would be good and a further 39.0% felt was necessary (see Table 8.3). However, with only 8.0% of staff considering such efforts are necessary and over one third of them having negative attitudes to physical activity, it hardly appears to be possible at this time. If talking and discussing such issues are to be worthwhile they must be related to more positive attitudes on the part of the staff who would be initiating any communication. Talking about exercise in many forms will facilitate the staff to appreciate the happier and more positive aspects of physical activity today and hopefully help them to overcome their fears of being forced to do it through the many different types of activity that are available in pleasant surroundings (Table 8.4).

The elderly, perhaps feeling the cold more because of poor circulation, also fear getting wet and cold (4.0%) whereas the staff do not raise this issue at all. Similarly, from past experience, they do not want to fall or get stuck and not be able to help themselves (4.0%). These are both fears that can be readily come to terms with through careful planning and progression by those responsible for elderly activity sessions be they recreational, rehabilitative or both. Those responsible for these sessions have a responsibility too to consider the fatigue factor carefully through adequate recovery in order to prevent the fears regarding getting tired, hurt or injured, or overdoing it becoming realities for the elderly and the staff. If the staff believe they have a duty to talk to the participants about activity then many of these inherent fears will be overcome and anxiety reduced for correct advice can be given at the appropriate time.

By far the most enjoyable activity experiece for the elderly is doing it in the warm. Wanting to do it is the main concern of the staff which is very much in keeping with their fears of being forced to participate above. 69.0% of the elderly enjoy what they want to do and choose to do and like doing it whereas only 47.0% of the staff who work with them are to be found in these groups. (Macheath 1982).

It can be readily observed from Table 8.5 that if the elderly are to be encouraged to paticipate in any form of physical activity there are some very clear guidelines as to what will make the experience pleasurable and thus repeated:-
(a)   It must be in the warm.
(b)   They must then want to do it.
(c)   It is in groups with friends.
(d)   They can choose what to do.
(e)   They must be able to manage it with not too much difficulty initially.

In addition Table 8.4 illustrates that those initiating such activities must ensure that:-

(a) There is a choice of activity.
(b) Initially it must not be too demanding.
(c) It must be set up so that success is assured with a modicum of effort in the early stages.
(d) Progress must be seen to be made - i.e. they can actually do it (Table 8.5).

It is important that the elderly feel secure in what they are doing and are not going to fall below the level of their peers. With proper planning this should present no problems for those responsible for activities for the elderly be they for recreational or rehabilitative purposes. Those planning such activities for their elderly patients, regardless of the circumstances, must take full cognizance of both the fears of the elderly and the aspects of participation that make activity an enjoyable undertaking. Only then will elderly participation and progress be positive and successful. These aspects of fear and pleasure can only be included if the staff talk to their elderly patients about exercise in order that they can be identified and the fears alleviated. But with only 21.0% and 8.0% of the staff respectively believing talking to the elderly about exercise is good and necessary, it is crucial that these people are assisted to develop more positive attitudes before they can in turn assist the elderly to come to terms with their fears.

OVERALL ATTITUDES TO ASPECTS OF EXERCISE

Approximately 33% of those staff working with the elderly in the Macheath (1982) study hold very negative views regarding talking to others about exercise; the same number believe elderly do not exercise at all; approximately 20% believe exercise to be negative and have a negative attitude to their own participation in such activities; and 20% fear being forced to take part in some form of physical exercise. These are the staff that are actually working with the elderly in the rehabilitative process who should be encouraging their elderly patients/clients to maintain their activities in order to keep their independence and freedom in the community.

The elderly individuals hold very different views on almost all the aspects of exercise discussed above. Their attitudes are positive regarding talking to others, believing that their peers do exercise and are better for it and that exercise is beneficial for them. They were naturally concerned about getting over tired or hurt.

Only when those staff working with the elderly in the Health, Education, and Social Services have a better understanding of the attitudes of the elderly to physical activity and its importance to them in the maintenance of their independence and freedom in the community along with the differences in their own attitudes to participation in such activities will the elderly be encouraged to take part, know what they should be able to do safely, and enjoy old age to the full.

Those involved in the rehabilitative and/or maintenance aspects of activity with the elderly have some clearly defined guidelines as to what will make participation purposeful and pleasurable; the types of advice needed for continued participation by the elderly and the importance the elderly place on exercise. With such positive attitudes to activity by the elderly those involved with them should make every effort to utilise this to the betterment of their independent existance in their communities.

Many elderly individuals realise that ageing has brought a decrease in physical activity but appreciated that this was not a good thing and felt the need for this to be pointed out to them (Macheath 1978).

Its muscle power if you haven't done exercise for years. They've gone lazy, haven't they?

That's the trouble, you get old and don't bother to use those muscles. You sit down with a book for hours and don't think no more about it, but when you come to discuss it you can appreciate it would be beneficial, especially the sitting ones (exercises).

You'd have to practice them, and be told them, you wouldn't think of them or be able to do them.

(Macheath 1978 p.146)

TABLE 8.1

Perceptions of Exercise by Group

More Positive Perceptions

	Staff %	Elderly* %
Good, right, excellent	36	23
Important	10	18
What all should do	3	5
Necessary, crucial, essential	4	5
What need, want	9	31
Help circulation, health	4	6
Working, keep fit	5	1
Keeping going	0	6
Beneficial	3	3
Relaxing	1	1
Helpful	1	6
Good in moderation	2	1

More Negative Perceptions

Only for youngsters	2	1
Only for the interested	4	0
Never done	1	1
Waste of time	0	6
Not for me, everyone	4	0
For those who want	3	1
Exhausted, hard work	4	0
What get here, all day	1	1
For fit ones	1	1

NB Some indicated more than one response

Source: Macheath, J A (1982)

TABLE 8.2

% Attitudes regarding talking to others
about Exercise by Group

	Staff %	Elderly* %
not done enough	15	52
good to do it	8	4
interesting/enlightening	5	1
should do more	4	14
important	7	14
necessary/needed/vital	6	21
helpful	0	4
done if need treatment	2	1
needs doing well	0	1
for staff to do	0	1
don't know what should do	2	14
only for those who know	4	1
part of job	2	0
pointless/daft	5	1
not for me/not on	6	0
not worthwhile/not good idea	5	2
awful/useless	4	0
unimportant/waste of time	14	1
hard work	1	0
feel tired	1	0
not my job	2	0

*includes more than one response in some cases

Source: Macheath, J A (1982)

TABLE 8.3

% Attitudes regarding elderly
who exercise by Group*

	<u>Staff</u> %	<u>Elderly*</u> %
keep fit/fitter for it	32	61
keep health/ier	5	20
do more things	1	12
have longer life	2	2
do well	6	16
happier/enjoy life	4	14
are few/rare	16	0
are sound in mind	2	0
don't/never do it	4	0
don't want to	1	0
mad/daft	2	0
can't	5	0
get tired/injured	1	0
are the healthier ones	1	4
are the fitter ones	11	5
are the younger ones	11	6
are the active ones	0.6	0.2
are lucky	0	4
are good at it	0.6	1
have done it all their lvies	4	9

*more than one response given in some cases

Source: Macheath, J A (1982)

117

TABLE 8.4

% fears regarding participation
in activity by Group*

	Staff %	Elderly* %
getting tired/exhausted	12	30
overdoing it/pushing too hard	19	19
getting hurt/injured	20	28
getting cold/wet	0	4
falling/getting stuck	2	4
aches and paines	0.6	4
not being able to do it	10	19
none	5	10
being forced to do it	20	9
running	0.6	0
doing what don't like	4	4
back/legs	1	0
not doing enough	0.6	0

*more than one response given in some cases

Source: Macheath, J A (1982)

TABLE 8.5

% reasons for enjoying activity
participation by group

	Staff %	Elderly* %
done in warm weather	17	34
done indoors	2	6
in groups/with friends	16	14
want to do it	30	42
can choose what do	8	14
like what doing	9	13
able to do it/fit to	2	8
do it easily	2	8
not too difficult	0	4
dressed property	0	2
done when want to	0	1
have time	4	0
make feel better	4	1
pain free	0.6	0
pleasant/can laugh	2	0
worthwhile	0.6	0
see benefits	0.6	0
not overdone	2	0
not forced to do it	8	6
competititive	0.6	0

*more than one response given in some cases

Source: Macheath, J A (1982)

119

Chapter Nine

THE UNDERSTANDING OF HEALTH AND GOOD PHYSICAL CONDITION

It has become apparent that individuals do not view exercise and fitness from the same standpoint. Nor do people of different ages view these contributors to health from the same standpoint. Each individual brings a very personal interpretation to her final concept which may reflect the results of the background experience and current situations of each and every individual.

With such a diversity of participation in many forms of social, physical, and leisure time pursuits illustrated in Chapter 4-7 above, one might expect the current understanding of health and physical condition to be equally diverse. Participation in those many and varied activities may well reflect the understanding of both health and good physical condition as a prerequisite for such participation.

Shanas et al (1968) suggests that subjective feelings are often much better indicators of the elderly individual's ability to function rather than the presence or absence of disease and particular medical conditions. The functioning of the elderly in the community is often related to their own perceptions of their health rather than their medically diagnosed health status (Rose and Peterson 1965). Abrams (1978) suggests that 40.0% of the elderly claim their health is good.

WHAT IS HEALTH?

The elderly relate health to their ability to do things and its importance to facilitating this. However, it is not the predetermined doing of specific tasks that is the major criterion, but the doing of tasks they actually wish to do. The staff of the Health, Education, and Social Services working with these elderly people, though, describe health in terms of learned factors of health (see Table 9.1). 41.0% of the elderly see health as important and everything they require whilst another 34.0% view health in terms of lifestyle - being independent, enjoying life, or doing what they wish to do. This is a very practical approach to health by the elderly, illustrating their whole person, non medical, and total lifestyle considerations that are affected purely by what they may wish to undertake at any given moment in time. In contrast, the staff assisting them in the rehabilitative/maintenance process see health purely in terms of food, exercise, rest, sound mind and body, and an absence of disease (39.0%). This follows closely the shopping list of health topics given by the Department of Education and Science (1968) of: "cleanliness; movement and rest; nutrition and food; warmth and clothing and care of the body". The elderly approach to health is much more akin to the view of health given by Wilson (1975) in suggesting that: "people choose what health, a healthy life means for them". Wilson (1975) goes on to suggest that: "health is situational, related to what people believe is a full life for them". The views of the staff are theoretical in nature and totally unrelated to their own needs and experience in direct opposition to the practical everyday approaches to health of their elderly patients with whom they work (Macheath 1982).

The staff also take a more clinical stance in regard to health. 12.0% see health as feeling well and a further 6.0% see health as being free from illness and disease. The elderly tend to accept many health problems as part of the ageing process (Shanas et al 1968) and not necessarily affecting their age adjusted lifestyle, or health to maintain that lifestyle. Supporting this elderly approach to health further 11.0% of this age group relate health to their ability to walk (can walk/able to walk). To most elderly, walking even very slowly is paramount to being independent and able to do what they wish to in their community.

Macheath (1978) found that the elderly saw health in functional terms or as a feeling of well being rather than a clinically related state. Function was related to their particular situation.

I can't do all my work so I'm not in good health.

It's what you make it. If you can do all you

want to that's good health.

(Macheath 1978).

This suggests that the health includes the ability to function in a given situation and appears also to be closely related to the lifestyle of the elderly. The feeling approach to health is much more subjective and may be governed by many different factors. "Its a wonderful feeling". "Its feeling great". (Macheath 1978). The 'feeling' approach appears to be an unattainable ideal for the majority of elderly who may then turn to the functional approach to health in order to rationalize or relieve frustration through not being able to attain such an ideal. The functional approach also includes the idea that walking is a health criterion for the elderly.

If walking is the crucial health factor for the elderly that it appears to be, it is of paramount importance that the SRNs, SENs and their Aides clearly understand this for they are the first of the rehabilitative health professionals to motivate the elderly sick towards returning to independence. All members of the Health, Education and Social Services need to appreciate that the elderly view health in totally different terms from themselves. It is the elderly individuals interpretation that the staff must use if they are to communicate with their elderly patients in terms that will be comprehended, remembered and acted upon - aspects that Fletcher (1972) suggests are vital for successful communication. If staff communicate their own 'shopping list' approach to health to the elderly, as reasons for doing particular activities independent practice will not be seen as important and progress will be inhibited for the elderly do not regard health in such terms and will not associate their needs with such a list.

WHAT IS GOOD PHYSICAL CONDITION?

One might assume that good health and good physical condition are both essential for an independent and free life in the community for people of all ages. However, it has been illustrated by Macheath (1982) in Table 9.1 that elderly people do see health in these functional terms but that the staff who work with them do not. Health status might also be considered to have an influence on physical condition for to participate in activity to improve one's physical condition may be said to depend on the current health status.

It is interesting to note in Table 9.2 the many different ways of inter-relating health and physical condition, but almost no one saw them as one and the same thing. Only 13.0% felt that health and physical condition were required. Three times more elderly than staff felt it was possible to have one's health without being in good physical condition, but only 1.0% of the staff and no elderly thought it possible to be in good physical condition and poor health. There is a feeling that physical condition involves physical activity and thus demands different criteria than health. Once again the whole life approach of the elderly is apparent. It is obvious that if they can get about, cope, and have some social life then they believe they are in good physical condition. This approach parallels their approach to health.

Good physical condition appears to require health as a prerequisite and to be allied to the use of the body to a greater extent in the Macheath (1978) study than in the 1982 investigation. The 1978 findings suggest that:-

> You've got to have your health before you can be in good physical condition
>
> (p127)

or

> Good physical condition is someone with sound body and limbs and doing everything you want to whether its work or enjoying yourself, or whatever
>
> (p128)

or

> Good physical condition means good for anything doesn't it. It means moving.
>
> (p128)

Health and good physical condition each have their own characteristics but in general terms the elderly tend to associate them with lifestyle and coping with their particular situation. Physical condition though also appears to be related to mobility and daily living activities.

> Legs are important, you need sensation in your legs. I can get down and do lots of things, but

then I pay for it later, therefore I am not in good physical condition.

(Macheath 1978 p128)

Good physical condition appears to be a more tangible concept for the elderly to discuss as they relate it to their ability to function at their desired level in the community. It is a pity that the staff who work with the elderly do not have the same positive approach to the assessment of necessary physical condition as their elderly patients. 3.0% of these groups believe that wheelchair bound individuals are not in good physical condition, regardless of the cause. What about the amputees, can they not be in good physical condition despite propelling themselves around in a wheelchair? What about the wheelchair bound who take part in the marathons and other such events now so much part of the current round of activities for all ages and sexes.

Once again the staff turn to the shopping list approach to defining good physical condition of the Department of Education and Science (1968) health topics. Right weight for height; well groomed; good mental condition and active mind. This approach to defining good physical condition appears to relate to training programme related materials and attitudes at the expense of their own experience and current situations.

As the staff believe one cannot have health if disease is present, 9.0% also believe one cannot have good physical condition without health (i.e. if have disease). The elderly appear to be very adaptable to the onset of problems they consider are related to ageing and because of their keeping busy and doing so gradually as rheumatism etc. creep insidiously upon them. The two approaches to the problems surrounding physical condition may be related to the tasks demanded of the staff and the elderly which differ considerably. However the staff do not see good physical condition in the same terms as they do health except in a general 'shopping list' approach. In contrast the elderly view health and good physical condition in similar terms, a fact which must be appreciated by the staff offering advice and encouragement to their elderly patients, be it on the wards, in the gymnasium, in an office, or in the community.

THE EFFECT OF EXERCISE ON HEALTH

Movement aids the maintenance and rehabilitation of general health (Gore 1973) and there is a strong correlation between activity levels and physical condition throughout old age (Bassey 1978). Physical activity is considered by the World Health Organization (1978) to be a positive health criterion whilst lack of such activity is considered a health risk.

Those showing positive attitudes to exercise (see Tables 8.1-8.3) in a variety of ways also have the same positive approaches to the effect of exercise on their health. 86.0% of the elderly believe exercise is necessary and indeed does have a positive effect on their health whereas only 33.0% of the staff in the Health, Education, and Social Services who work with these elderly people hold such views (Table 9.3). Another 11.0% of the elderly believe exercise has an effect on keeping their limbs going and therefore keeping them mobile. It is amazing to see that 8.0% of these staff do not see exercise as necessary whilst 3.0% of the elderly (all virtually bedfast from strokes) cannot exercise but do see themselves as healthy.

These ideas regarding the effects of exercise on health do indeed follow the general trend that is emerging. There are very different concepts of health, good physical condition, and the effects of exercise on health between the elderly and their helpers (i.e. the staff). There is a relationship between the concepts of the three areas though within those termed the elderly and those termed the staff in Tables 9.1-9.3. On the one hand the elderly have very positive, whole person lifestyle needs approaches to the three aspects but those purporting to assist them in the rehabilitation and maintenance of their independence in the community have more negative, shopping list, unrelated to lifestyle approaches to health, good physical condition and the effects of exercise on them.

It is surprising that only 22.0% of the staff believe physical activity is helpful or beneficial to health whilst just 3.0% see it as essential or important. If so few of the nursing and other hospital orientated caring Health professions consider that physical activity has any positive effect on health, the elderly patients in their charge are not going to be encouraged to 'get up and go' or indeed to walk following spells of inactivity in bed as part of the rehabilitative process. Walking is a basic form of exercise that the elderly prize (Table 9.1) for it is crucial to their being able to get around and do things for themselves, that can be done in a small area despite a low fitness level. However, if the staff fail to see exercise as important and communicate this to their patients, the motive for rehabilitation and future life in the community may quickly fade and the elderly instead of improving physically will lose that basic level of strength and fitness required for even the basic daily living activities.

The elderly generally believe that exercise is beneficial to health and keeps them going in relation to their particular lifestyle. Again Macheath (1978) provides supporting evidence of this approach to exercise and health. The effects of exercise on the body are expressed in a wide variety of ways reflecting past experience and also a lack of knowledge of body function, e.g.

> It freshens up the body all the time, it slackens the outside skin and allows it to get around the bones on your body, which feeds the bones to make them stronger.

The elderly are obsessed with being able to walk and use this medium on occasion to express their views on the effects of exercise on health.

> It does you good to just get up and walk around, even if it's just round the flat. If you don't, you don't get your circulation going.
>
> (Macheath 1978 p132)

Comments:
It has been become clear that the elderly have a very different understanding of health, good physical condition and the role of exercise in these from the staff in the Health, Education, and Social Services who work with them. With the very negative attitudes of the staff regarding exercise (outlined in Chapter 8) perhaps one should not be surprised that their understanding of health and physical condition follow similar trends. The important factor is not that such diversities exist bewteen the staff and their elderly patients but that these differences are identified and comprehended.

In order for these staff to be able to offer appropriately structured advice to the elderly regarding their rehabilitation towards returning to the community or maintaining their independence it is important that they appreciate the existance of differences between them and their patients. Having appreciated this, any advice offered must be couched not in the attitudes of the staff but in the attitudes of their elderly patients if they are to be successfully received.

The beliefs of the staff regarding the effects of exercise on health may even mitigate against positive suggestions being offered to the elderly patients despite the elderly themselves seeing exercise as beneficial to their health. Couple this with the 'shopping list' approach of the staff to health and the 'no disease' 'don't see the doctor' approach to physical condition and one wonders where such staff will begin to cross the great divide between them and their elderly patients.

Both health and good physical condition are necessary in order that the elderly can lead independent and free lifestyles in the community. If one of these components falls too low the quality of life will be impaired. The concepts discussed above support the importance of mobility (especially walking) to the elderly as an indication of their health and general physical condition.

It is apparent that all staff working with the elderly, be it in the hospital, club, home or community, will require a great deal of assistance to come to terms with the differences in concepts of health and good physical condition between them and the elderly.

The current generation of elderly appear to accept readily whatever happens and adapt to it, taking moderate disease, illness, and deformity as the natural stages of passing through old age. Their overall holistic approach to health and physical condition may be the result of their past experiences of a hardworking youth, making do through the two world wars and the depression, and the absence of modern conveniences for the home and transport in their early years. The current generation of elderly were certainly the product of different lifestyles in their youth from the staff who work with them. It may be these differences that are the basis for the different approaches to health, exercise and physical condition today. The reasons behind such differences need consideration in order that staff can be prepared for future generations of elderly in similar terms.

Health was seen as a component of good physical condition, although generally the reverse was not the case, and exercise was seen as beneficial to health particulary in the functional approach. Many elderly felt better as a result of exercise, especially in relation to stiffness and leg movements. The elderly feel that circulation is improved by activity thus supporting the view of Nateef (1960) and all were agreed that exercise led to a good feeling of well being in relation to the subjective concept of health expressed earlier.

The concepts of health and physical condition were perceived as separate and not interchangeable as suggested by Baumann (1961). Macheath (1978) suggests that the elderly see the social importance of exercise and the greater engagement it brought as beneficial to their overall well being.

There appears to be a correlation between the positive concepts of health, good physical condition, the affects of exercise on health and the attitudes to exercise outlined in Chapter 8. The elderly clearly see exercise as a beneficial and important contribution to health, independence and a reasonable lifestyle.

TABLE 9.1

% Understanding of Health by Group*

	Staff	Elderly
got all there is/got everything	10.0	24
good thing/important	8.0	23
doing what you want	2.0	12
keep busy/doing things	0.6	3
doing everything/being independent	1.0	14
feeling/well/fit/fit outlook	12.0	4
no disease/free from illness	6.0	3
enjoy life/full life	6.0	5
no aches and pains/no complaints	2.0	2
luck	2.0	0
not worrying about health	0.6	0
good appetite/eating right food	13.0	3
exercise/walking	7.0	1
rest/sleep	2.0	0
can walk/able to	1.0	11
sound mind/body	9.0	4
attitude of mind	2.0	1
depends on individual	2.0	0
watch weight/not overeating	2.0	0
not breathless	2.0	0
keep fit and active	6.0	2

* in some cases more than one response was given

Source: Macheath, J A (1982)

TABLE 9.2

% Understanding of Good Physical Condition
by Group

	Staff	Elderly
need health and physical condition	12.0	14.0
can't have physical condition without health	9.0	0.6
can have health and not physical condition	6.0	18.0
fitness and physical condition are the same	0.0	0.6
can have physical condition and not health	1.0	0.0
physical condition is related to athletics	1.0	0.0
if physical condition is good, health is good	4.0	2.0
capable of doing/able to cope	7.0	18.0
doing what can	0.0	8.0
good social life/enjoying self	7.0	18.0
keeping active	2.0	2.0
walking on own/plenty of walking	0.6	2.0
don't see doctor	0.6	0.0
not in physical condition if in wheelchair	3.0	0.0
right weight/for height	1.0	0.0
well groomed	0.6	0.0
no aches and pains	0.6	0.0
healthy body using limbs	0.6	0.0
good mental condition/active mind	4.0	0.0
not worrying about physical condition	0.6	0.0

* in some cases more than one response was given

Source: Macheath, J A (1982)

TABLE 9.3

% Understanding of the Effects of Exercises
on Health by Group

	Staff	Elderly
exercise should help health		
helps a lot/beneficial	22.0	56.0
very good	8.0	28.0
essential/important	3.0	2.0
keeps limbs going/get aches and pains if don't	1.0	11.0
helps sometimes	1.0	0.0
all depends/depends on individual	3.0	0.0
helps brain/ mind	2.0	0.0
feel exhilirated	1.0	0.0
not really help	6.0	0.6
can't do any but am healthy	0.0	3.0
normal activity all that's needed	1.0	
not jogging	0.6	
makes me ill	0.6	

* in some cases more than one response was given

Source: Macheath, J A (1982)

Chapter Ten

THE FUTURE AND ITS NEEDS - SUMMARY AND CONCLUSIONS

In many instances the current generation of elderly people, both men and women, have greater participation levels in any leisure time activities than the younger generations with only a modest decline in the over eighties age group. Despite the mobility problems raised by Shanas et al (1968), Abrams (1978) and Age Concern (1974/1977), Table 10.1 clearly demonstrates that the elderly in the Macheath (1982) District Health Authority do get out and about, and indeed are as active if not more so, as the younger staff with whom they come into contact. The over eighty year olds compare very favourably with the under forty year olds.

It must be remembered that the current generations of elderly are a highly selective, exclusive group having survived disease in their youth (smallpox, diphtheria, etc), two world wars and the depression which have taken their toll on many of their peers. The current elderly have character, determination, the ability to overcome adversity and a background of frugal living in their early years. They are used to being independent, doing things for themselves and getting themselves about. Future generations of elderly will not have this life experience to fall back on.

If the under sixty year olds are so inactive now, are they going to take up activities such as walking on retirement which the current generation of elderly have done all their lives? Will the inactivity of the under forty year olds reflect in their activity patterns throughout their lives? Further longitudinal studies are required to furnish the answers to these questions in order that future advice for all sections of society may be realistically planned with their longevity in mind.

The over eighty year olds have equally positive

beliefs regarding the physical activity of their peers. In almost all the activities listed in Table 10.2 there is a marked increase in the belief levels that older people participate in activities around retirement age.

Only in three activities (gardening, dancing and bowls) do the belief levels of elderly participation even reach the 40.0% level. In contrast only in billiards (40.0% and 45.0% respectively) does the belief level of the 60-79 and over 80 years age group and cycling (48.0%) in the latter age group, drop below the 60.0% level. This overall picture raises some real areas of concern for those responsible for the rehabilitation and maintenance of independent services and their staff.

If the younger people do not believe the elderly participate in physically demanding activities into and throughout old age, they certainly are not going to spend time encouraging them to actually get involved in the course of their work. Such a negative approach on the part of the staff who work with the elderly will be reflected in the attitudes they display to their patients regarding any form of physical activity. The advice offered will fail to present information in positive terms, related to their patients' understanding of physical activity patterns pertaining to themselves and their peers. It appears that In-Service training is urgently needed to rectify this situation.

Similarly, if these same younger generations of staff feel that talking about physical activities in any form is of such little value (see Chapter 8) it will further limit discussion taking place, especially in the hospital situation where they also believe that most elderly people are inactive and just sit watching the television screen most of the day (see Chapter 7). If any elderly individuals currently taking up hospital beds through illness and/or injury are to be encouraged to return to the level of fitness required to become resident in the community once more, it appears that attitude change must take place in the younger generations of staff working with them. As a result, many elderly people gradually decline in strength and fitness, becoming invalids, losing their independence and freedom, when with but a little encouragement and assistance they could enjoy the future in their own community.

While the staff hold the DES (1968) shopping list approach to the understanding of health and good physical condition and the elderly hold the Wilson (1975) situational approach to health it will be difficult for communication and joint understanding of basic philosophies truly to occur. Any advice that is offered will be ineffectual and fail to make its message understood unless clearly related to the elderly individual in his/her current situation. The elderly have a positive approach to exercise and health that is refreshing to witness. The younger generations of staff who work with them seem to have failed to grasp the interrelationship of health, exercise and living in the community in old age. Such negative approaches to these areas require rectifying before it is too late in order that lifetime activities may be evolved and developed well before their own old age is achieved.

There is clearly a relationship between participation in physical activities of daily living and leisuretime, positive overall attitudes to exercise relative to the individual environment of the elderly and positive attitudes to health. If future generations of elderly are to be as active as the current generation of British elderly and hold similar positive whole person environment related concepts of health, the current younger generations needs a great deal of assistance and positive encouragement now.

The elderly believe they and their peers are busy much of the day; are not only involved in the more physical pursuits, but also the hobbies that are productive; are involved in listening to the radio, watching television and reading; and also shopping, visiting friends and relations, going to Clubs and pubs. The current generation of elderly people have always been used to being active and busy, especially in their earlier years when modern technology was not available. It is these lifetime habits that are reflected in their lifestyles, attitudes and beliefs today.

Those in the under forty years age group have had the benefits of modern technology, including the car, for the greater part of their lives. Television, being new in the late 1950s, replaced crafts and self entertainment for most adolescents and younger adults. These early adult leisure time pursuits and trends are apparent in the attitudes to exercise, leisure time activities and estimates of what elderly people do. It is apparent that those who have positive attitudes to exercise, coupled with positive views of health and good physical condition regardless of age, also believe that the elderly are capable of physical activity and do not spend their time vegetating before the television set.

The elderly do not see themselves or their peers as inactive or incapable, but as people with a variety of interests and activities often based on lifetime interests.

There is a marked difference in the understanding of activity patterns in old age between the elderly themselves and those staff in the Health, Education and Social Services who work with them. There are also marked differences in the actual participation levels of these two groups with the elderly much more prone to be involved in a wide range of activities.

A correlation between the belief levels regarding activity in old age and the actual participation in physical activity is noticeable. There is also a correlation between the staff professional qualifications, activity participation levels and beliefs of activity participation by the elderly. Do these differing attitudes stem from the different training programmes for the various professionals or do they stem from contact with the elderly in the community?

Such misconceptions regarding physical activities in old age preclude appropriate, positive, advice and encouragement being given to the elderly by those involved in the rehabilitation of the elderly or their maintenance in the community.

Staff require Health Education themselves at two levels:

(a) their own participation in physical activity now as future generations of elderly

(b) the importance of the role of physical activity in the maintenance of independence and freedom throughout old age.

In addition, all the staff working with the elderly in the various situations need advice on the activity patterns of the elderly and the social reasons behind these activity patterns. Only then will the staff be capable of presenting relevant and realistic advice to their elderly patients. This Health Education advice for the staff regarding physical activities for both themselves and their elderly patients must be based upon knowledge of the background of the participants and thus must be adjusted and related to each group.

It is suggested that through the provision of a variety of suitable courses, particularly related to physical activity, as an integral part of In-Service training for all staff working with the elderly, it is possible for these staff to offer appropriate, positive advice in realistic terms to their elderly patients that is based upon understanding and knowledge. As future generations of elderly people increase in number, and the concepts of fitness develop in relation to the social mores of the future, further research will be needed into the patterns of physical activity of the elderly in order that cognizance may be taken of them. Only then will the staff of the Health, Education, and Social Services working with future generations of elderly people be able to offer advice to them that is realistic, relevant and based upon the most recent knowledge and understanding of physical activity patterns in old age that are available. It is only through regular research that future generations of the elderly will be positively assisted to maintain and regain their prized independence and freedom in the community in which they live and enjoy leading full and worthwhile lives into and throughout old age.

Should the results of the Macheath (1982) study be repeated in other District Health Authorities in other parts of the country be repeated with different populations of elderly, then those responsible for the training of personnel in the branches of the Health, Education, and Social Services involved with the elderly, must plan and provide relevant training programmes to assist these staff to improve their understanding of what the elderly actually do and believe that they and their peers do. Similar research is urgently required with the many ethnic groups that also have members reaching retirement age for their activities and beliefs may differ greatly from those of the Macheath (1978 and 1982) studies conducted in south east Kent.

This text has highlighted some of the problems, differences and areas of concern pertaining to physical activity in old age and the current generation of elderly. These people had a more puritan upbringing that did not include the modern conveniences available today. The investigation will need to be repeated with each subsequent generation of elderly in order that these staff in the Health, Education and Social Services will comprehend the situation and be well prepared to offer appropriate advice regarding health, rehabilitation, activity and ageing. Only then will the current and future generations be prepared to enjoy to the full their independence and freedom in their own community into and throughout their old age in relation to their individually chosen life style.

TABLE 10.1

% Participation in Activity by Age

	Age Groups			
	Under 40	40-59	60-79	Over 80 years
Attend Club Regularly	13	12	57	42
Swim Regularly	16	8	56	16
Walk Regularly	43	56	93	85
Garden Occasionally	39	66	51	20
Knit Regularly	23	48	46	25
Knit Occasionally	22	22	20	25
Sew Regularly	10	33	30	24
Sew Occasionally	43	34	35	44

Source: Macheath, J A (1982)

TABLE 10.2

% Believing Elderly Participate
in Activities by Age

	Age Groups			
	Under 40	40-59	60-79	Over 80 years
Housework daily	26	37	87	70
Shop for food daily	22	37	91	84
Occasional holiday	34	50	96	90
Pub regularly	30	34	82	72
Sporting event occasionally	36	45	76	72
Swim regularly	11	23	69	33
Walk regularly	22	44	87	93
Golf occasionally	17	20	83	80
Cycle occasionally	18	20	82	48
Bowls occasionally	46	61	100	97
Dance occasionally	41	51	88	90
Billiards regularly	12	22	40	45
Darts regularly	15	29	63	75
Woodwork occasionally	28	28	74	92
D I Y occasionally	28	28	74	92
Painting occasionally	32	28	68	64
Garden occasionally	42	63	89	95
Eat out occasionally	28	40	84	92

Source: Macheath, J A (1982)

BIBLIOGRAPHY

Abel Smith B. & Townsend, P. (1965) The Poor and
the Poorest, Bell: London
Abercrombie, M. (1974) Aims and techniques of Group
Discussion. Social Research in Education:
London
Abrams, M. (1978) Beyond Three Score Ten 1, Age
Concern: London
Abrams, M. (1980) Beyond Three Score Ten 11, Age
Concern: London
Abramson, J.H. (1974) Survey Methods in Community
Medicine, Churchill Livingstone: Edinburgh.
Adams, G. (1970) Some Observations on the Training
Programme and Setting, in Gitman, L. & Woodford,
Williams, E. (1970) Research, Training and
Practice in Clinical Medicine of Ageing, Basle:
Kaeger
Administration on Ageing (1975) The Fitness Challenge
in Later Years, Washington: H.E.W.
Agate, J. (1972) Geriatrics for Nurses, Heinemann:
London
Age Concern (1972) Easing the Restrictions of Ageing,
Age Concern: London
Age Concern (1977) Profiles of the Elderly 1,2,3
and 5, Age Concern: London
Age Concern (1974) Attitudes of the Elderly, Age
Concern: London
Allman, F & Watt, E. (1970) Role of Exercise in
Disease Prevention, in Allman, F. and Ryan,
A. (1970) Sports Medicine: New York Academic
Press
American Medical Association & A.A.H.P.E.R. (1964)
Exercise and Fitness, J.O.P.H.E.R.
Anderson, J. & Day, J. (1968) New Self administered
medicine questionary, British Medical Journal
4:636
Anderson, N. (1961) Work and Leisure, Routledge

& Kegan Paul: London

Anderson, W.F. (1970) Geriatrics: A speciality, in Gitman, L and Woodford Williams, E. (197) Research, Training and Practice in Clinical Medicine of Ageing, Basle: Kaeger

Anderson, W.F. (1976) The Growth of Geriatric Medicine, in Britsh Geriatric Society (1974) Doctors and Old Age, British Geriatric Society

Anderson, W.F. (1973) The Health needs of the elderly, in Carvin, R. and Person, N. (1973) Needs of the Elderly, University of Exeter

Anderson, W.F. (1972) Preventive Aspects of Geriatric Medicine, Postgrad. Med.Journ.

Anderson, W.F. (1976) Preventive Aspects of Geriatric Medicine, Physiotherapy 62:15

Anderson, W.F. (1955) A consultative health centre for older people, Lancet, 2:239

Anderson, W.F. (1976) Geriatric medicine, an academic approach, Age and Ageing, 5:4

Angeleu, J. (1965) Problems of Accommodation and Medico social care of old people, Strasburg: Council of Europe

Antonini, F.M. (1970) Training for the practice of Clinical Gerontology; Requirements of a training programme, in Gitman, L. and Woodford Williams, E. (1970) Research Training and Practice in Clinical Medicine of Ageing, Basle: Kaeger

Arie, T. (1973) Psychiatric Needs of the Elderly in Canvin, R. and Pearson, N. (1973) Needs of the Elderly, University of Exeter

Arie, T. (1973) Doctors, medical students and psycho-geriatrics, Mod. Geriatrics, 6, 1973

Arkley, J. (1964) The Over 60s, Nat. Council for Social Services: London

Atkinson, A.B. (1973) Financial Needs of the Elderly, in Canvin, R. and Pearson, N. (1973) Needs of the Elderly, University of Exeter

Bainbridge, C. (1971) Planning a Geriatric Services, Geriatrics, 3:227-232

Ball, J. (1971) Health Education Lessons for Primary Schools, Journ. Centre Ed. for Development Overseas, 5:4

Barber, G. (1973) Country Doctor, Boydell, Ipswich

Bassey, J. (1978) Age, Inactivity and some physiological responses to exercise, Gerontology 24:66-77

Baumann, B. (1961) Diversity of Concepts of Health and Physical Fitness, Journal Health & Human Behaviour, 2

Beattie, A. (1977) The planning of preventive services for the elderly, unpublished thesis, M.Med.Sci. University of Nottingham

de Beavoir, S. (1972) Old Age, Deutch
Bennett, A.E. and Ritchie, K. (1977) Questionnaires
    in Medicine, O.U.P.: London
Berger, P. & B. (1972) Sociology, a biographical
    approach, Penguin: London
Bernstein, B. (1975) Class, Code and Control, R.K.P.:
    London
Berrington Jones, N. (1975) Activities for the Elderly,
    Journal Royal Society of Health 75:2, 96-98
Bigor, A. (1974) The Relevance of American Life
    Satisfaction Indicies for research on British
    subjects before and after retirement, Age and
    Ageing, 3
Birren, J. (1959) Handbook of the Ageing Individual,
    Chicago
Boreham, M. (1977) The use of case histories to
    assess the nurses ability to solve clinical
    problems, Journal Advanced Nursing, 2
Bortz, E. (1960) Exercise and Fitness in Ageing,
    in Staley, S. (196) Exercise and Fitness, Illinois:
    Amer. Coll. Sports Med.
Bosanquet, N. (1968) A Future Old Age New Society
Boyle, C. (1970) Differences between patients and
    doctors interpretations of some common medical
    terms, in Cox, C. and Mead, A. (1970) A Sociology
    of Medical Practice, Macmillan: London.
Brearley, P. (1978) Ageing and Social Work, in Hobman.
    D. (ed) 1978) The Social Challenge of Ageing,
    Croom Helm: London
Bracey, H. (1966) In Retirement, R.K.P.: London
British Geriatric Society (1976) Doctors and Old
    Age, British Geriatric Society: London
British Life Assurance Tract & British Medical Assoc-
    iation, (1976). The Next Twenty Years, BLAT/BMA:
    London
Brocklehurst, J. (1978) Ageing and Health, in Hobman,
    D. (ed) (1978) The Social Challenge of Ageing,
    Croom Helm: London
Brocklehurst, J. (1973) Textbook of Geriatric Medicine
    and Gerontology, Churchill: London
Brocklehurst, J. (1974) Educational Opportunities
    in Geriatric Medicine, Age and Ageing, 3:3
Brocklehurst, J. (1972) The Way Ahead, Age and Ageing,
    1:3
Bromley, D. (1972) The Psychology of Ageing, Penguin:
    London
Brouha, L. (1966) Physiology of Training including
    age and sex differences, in Slusher, A. and
    Lockhart, A. (1966) Authology of Contemporary
    Readings - An Introduction to Physical Education,
    Iowa: Brown

141

Brown, R.S.G. (1973) The Changing National Health
     Service, R.K.P.: London
Bruner, B. (1960) The effect of Physical Exercise
     on metabolic potential: A crucial measure of
     physical potential, in Staley, S. (1960) Exercise
     and Fitness, Illinois: American Coll.Sports.Med.
Bruner, B. and Joki, E. (1970) Physical Activity
     and Ageing, Basle: Kaeger
Burgess, J. (1960) Ageing in Western Culture, Univ.
     Chicago
Butterworth, E. and Holman, R. (1975) Social Welfare
     in Modern Britain, Fontana: London
Byrne, P. and Lang, B. (1976) Doctors Talking to
     Patients, H.M.S.O.: London
Canvin, R. and Pearson, N. (1973) Needs of the Elderly,
     University of Exeter
Carmichael, R. (1978) The Practical Problems met
     in Tapping Voluntary Resources Available, Journ.
     Royal Society of Health, 5
Carver, V. & Liddiard, P. (1978) An Ageing Population,
     Hodder and Stoughton: London
C.S.O. (1976) Social Trends, H.M.S.O.: London
Central Office of Information, (1977) Care of the
     Elderly in Britain, H.M.S.O.: London
Choice (1978) Retirement Briefing File, Choice:
     London
Chown, S. (ed) (1972) Human Ageing, Penguin: London
Clarke, H. (1966) Contributions of Physical Education
     to Physical Fitness in Slusher, H. and Lockhart,
     A. (1966) Authology of Contemprary Readings
     - An Introduction to Physical Education, Brown:
     Iowa
Clarke, W. (1978) Optimizing Voluntary Effort, Journ.
     Royal Society of Health, 5
Cleugh, M. (1962) Educating Older People, Tavistock:
     London
Cochrane, A.L. (1973) Screening the Elderly in Canvin,
     R. and Pearson, N. Needs of the Elderly, University
     of Exeter
Colin-Russ, E. (1975) Reorganisation towards an
     evaluation, First Impressions, Royal Society
     of Health: London
Confrey, E. & Goldstein, N. (1964) The Health Status
     of Older People, in Tibbetts, C. (1964) Handbook
     of Social Gerontology: Chicago
Cortazzi, D. & Roote, S. (1978) Illuminative Incident
     Analysis, McGraw Hill: N.Y.
Cowan, N. (1971) Preventive Aspects of Geriatric
     Medicine, Modern Geriatrics, 269-281
Cumming & Henry (1961) Growing Old, Basic: N.Y.
Cunningham, D.A. et.al. (1968) Active Leisuretime

activities as related to use among males in
the total population, Journ. Gerontology 23:551-6
Cureton, T. (1960) Anatomical Psysiological, Psycho-
logical Changes induced by Exercise in Staley,
S. (1960) Exercise, Sport and Games in Adults,
Illinois: Amer. Coll. Sports. Med.
Datta, S. (1973) A training programme in geriatric
medicine, Mod. Geriatrics, 6
Davie, L. (1979) Health Practices Study, Clin.S.
California
D.E.S. (1968) Handbook of Health Education, H.M.S.O.:
London
Dept. H.E.W. (1979) A directory of expanding role
programmes for registered nurses, H.E.W.:
Washington
Dept. H.E.W. The Challenge of Fitness in Later Years,
H.E.W.: Washington
D.H.S.S. (1977) Prevention and Health, H.M.S.O.:
London
D.H.S.S. (1978) A Happier Old Age, H.M.S.O.: London
D.H.S.S. (1976) The State of Public Health, H.M.S.O.:
London
D.H.S.S. (1974) Medical Staffing in the N.H.S.
in England and Wales, Health Trends, 6:2
D.H.S.S. (1977) Career Prospects for established
Registrars of obtaining a senior registrar
post, Health Trends, 9
D.H.S.S. (1977) Medical staffing and prospects in
the N.H.S. in England and Wales in 1976, Health
Trends, 9
D.H.S.S. (1977) Prevention and Health, H.M.S.O.:
London
D.H.S.S. (1972) Department of Health and Social
Services Annual Report, 1971, H.M.S.O.: London
Downs, H. (1979) 30 Dirty Lies about Old, Argus:
Illinois
Draper, P. et.al. (1977) Health and Wealth, Journ.
Royal Society of Health, 7:3
Drinkwater, B. (1960) Development of an Attitude
Inventory to measure the attitudes of High
School Girls towards Physical Education as
a career for women, Research Quarterly, 31:
575-580
Dubos, R. (1970) Man, Medicine and the Environment,
Penguin: London
Elder, G. (1977) The Alienated - Growing Old Today,
Redwood Burn: London
Elliott, J. (1975) Living in Hospital, King Edward
Hospital Fund: London
Elliot, R. (1966) Centres for joint use by family
doctors and health department staff, Journ.

Royal Society of Health, 5

Ellis, J. (1979) The selection of medical students, Health Trends, 11

Exton Smith, A. and Stanton, B. (1975) Report on dietary of elderly woman living alone, King Edward Hospital Fund: London

Fairnsworth, T. (1977) Getting through to your patient, Pulse, 30:7

Fentem, P. (1976) Vibration BP and Heart Rate, Physiotherapy, 63;11

Fentem, P. and Bassey, J. (1978) The Case for Exercise, The Sports Council

Fixx, J. (1977) The Complete Book of Running, Random House: N.Y.

Fletcher, C.M. (1972) Communication in Medicine, Nuffield Provincial Hospital Trust: London

Foren, R. and Brown, M. (1971) Planning for Services, Knight: London

Francis, G. (1973) Caring for the Elderly, Heinemann: London

Freeman, J.T. (1972) Medical School Education in Geriatrics in Blumenthal, H.T. (ed) Medical and Clinical Aspects of Ageing, Columbia: N.Y.

Fullarton, S. (1978) When a man's best friend is his hobby, Woman's Own

Gagne, R. (1970) Learning theory, educational media and individualised instruction, Educational Broadcasting Review, 4, 49-62

Gale, J. and Livesey, B. (1974) Attitudes towards Geriatrics - A report of the Kings Survey, Age and Ageing, 3:49

Gillet, C. (1971) Connexions, All in the Game, Penguin: London

Gitman, L. and Woodford Williams, E. (1970) Research, Training and Practice in Clincial Medcine of Ageing, Kaeger: Basle

Goldberg, M. (1970) Helping the Aged: A field experiment in social work, Allen and Unwin: London

Gordon, R. (1980) Interviewing: Strategy Techniques and Tactics, Dorsey: Illinois

Gore, I. (1973) Ageing and Vitality, Allen and Unwin

Gore, I. (1978) Social Attitudes to old age - exploding the myth, Mod. Geriatrics, 11

Gore, I. (1977) Don't ask "How old are you" ask them "How fit are you?" Mod. Geriatrics, 1

Green, L. (1977) Education and Measurement some dilemmas for Health Education, Amer. Journ. Public Health, 67:2, 156-162

Griffiths, G. (1958) The Needs of old people in Rural Areas, Journal Royal Society of Health, 4

Grossman, J. et.al. (1971) Evaluation of Computer

acquired patient history, JAMA 215:1286

Halsey, A. (1972) Trends in British Society since 1980, Macmillan: London

Harrel, G. (1970) Training for Practice in Clincial Gerontology: The training programme and the settling in Gitman, H. and Woodford Williams E. (1970) Research, Training and Practice in Clinical Medicine of Ageing, Kaeger: Basle

Harris, R. (1970) Some observations on Geriatrics as a Speciality in Gitman, L. and Woodford Williams, E. (1970) Research, Training and Practice in Clinical Medicine of Ageing, Kaeger: Basle

Hatch, S. (1978) Volunteers, Mutual Aid and Health, Journal Royal Society of Health, 5

Havighurst, R. (1978) Ageing in Western Society in Hobman, D. (1978) The Social Challenge of Ageing, Croom Helm: London

Hawker, M. (1974) Geriatrics for Physiotherapists and allied professions, Faber: London

Hawker, M. (1978) Remedial Helpers, Department of Geriatrics, Edgware General Hospital: London

Hazell, K. (1960) Social and Medical Problems of the elderly, Hutchinson: London

H.E.C./Scot. H.Ed.Dept. (1979) Look After Yourself, H.E.C.: London

H.E.C./Sports Council, (1977) Everyday Health and Fitness, H.E.C.: London

H.E.C./Scot. H.Ed. Dept. (1978) Feeling Great, H.E.C.: London

H.E.W. (1978) The Fitness Challenge in Later Years, H.E.W.: Washington

Hearnshaw, L. (1972) Work and Age, Age and Ageing, 1:81

Hill, W. (1969) Learning through discussion, Ca: Sage

Hinds, S. (1973) The Personal & Sociomedical aspects of Retirement, Journal Royal Society of Health, 83:6, 281-286

Hobman, D. (ed) (1978) The Social Challenge of Ageing, Croom Helm: London

Hobson, W. and Pemberton, J. (1965) Health of the Elderly at Home, Butterworth: London

Hochbaum, G.A. (1971) Measurement of effectiveness in Health Education attitudes, Journal of Health Education, 14(1) 54-59

Hodkinson, H. (1975) An outline of Geriatrics, Academic: N.Y.

Holding, D. (1965) Principles of Training, Pergamon: London

Holland, W. (1977) Foreword in Bennett, A.E. and

Ritchie, K. (1977) Questionnaires in Medicine,
O.U.P.: London
Home Office (1968) The Report of the Committee on
Local Authority and Allied Personal Social
Services (Seebohm Report) H.M.S.O.: London
Hooker, S. (1976) Caring for the Elderly People,
R.K.P.: London
Hooper, R. (1971) The Curriculum: Context, Design
and Development, Oliver and Boyd: London
Haworth, J.T. and Smith, M. (1975) Work and Leisure,
Macmillan: London
Howell, T. (1974) Origins of the British Geriatric
Society, Age and Ageing, 3:2
Hunt, A. (1978) The Elderly at Home, H.M.S.O.:
London
Hurd, G. (1973) Human Societies, R.K.P.: London
Illich, I. (1975) Medical Nemesis, Penguin: London
Isaacs, B. and Neville, Y. (1976) The Management
of Need in the Elderly, Scot. Dept. Health
Education: Edinburgh
Ivey, T. Tso, and Stamm, M. (1975) Communication
Techniques for Patient Instruction, Amer. Journ.
Hospital Pharmacy, 32: 828-831
Jacob, J. (1975) Older Persons and Retirement Commun-
ities, Thomas: Illinois
Johnson, M. (1978) Social Attitudes to Old Age exploding
the myth Mod. Geriatrics 11
Kane, J. (1974) Physical Education in Secondary
Schools, Macmillan: London
Kastenbaum, R. (1979) Growing Old - Years of Fulfilment,
Harper Row: London
Kinnie, A. & Arnott, M. (1973) The Quality of Life
in Glasgow's East End, Age and Ageing, 2:46
Knapp, M. (1976) Prediciting the dimension of life
satisfaction, Journ. Gerontology, 31:5
Kupst et.al. (1975) Evaluation of methods to improve
communication in the Physician-Patient Relation-
ships, American Journal Orth.Physch, 45:3
Larrabee, E. & Meyersohn (1958) Mass Leisure, Free
Press: Illinois
Larson, L. (1961) Health and Fitness in the World,
American Inst. Amer.Coll. Sports. Med.: Illinois
Larson, L. and Michaelson, H. (1973) International
Guide to Fitness and Health, Crown: N.Y.
Lewis, B. and Oldfield, C. (1977) The Maintenance
of the Elderly in the Community, Ciceley Northcote
Trust: London
Leslie, J. (1977) Nutrition and Diet of the Elderly,
Nursing Mirror, 25/8
Ley, P. (1972) Comprehension in memory and the success
of communication with the patient, Journ.Inst.

of Health Ed. 10
Ley, P. and Spelman, M. (1973) Communicating with
    the Patient, Staple: London
Logan, R.F. (1970) The Aged in Britain in Gitman, L.
    and Woodford Williams E. (1970) Research, Training
    and Practice in Clinical Medicine of Ageing,
    Kaeger: Basle
Loshak, D. (1978) Daily Telegraph Guide to Retirement,
    Collins: London
Loving, B. (1975) Why we must act to diffuse the
    age explosion, Choice: London
Lowry, L. (1979) Social Work with the Ageing, Harper
    Row: London
Mack, M.B. (1977) Rehabilitation of cardiac elderly
    handicapped by biasses, Geriatrics, 122-3
Macheath, J.A. (1978) Concepts of fitness in the
    elderly - A study of activity levels and attitudes
    to exercise in voluntary groups attending Clubs,
    unpublished M.Sc. thesis, University of London
Macheath, J.A. (1982) A study of the need and provision
    for Health Education in the training of profess-
    ionals that work with the elderly, with special
    reference to physical activity and fitness
    in old age, Unpublished PhD thesis, University
    of London
Macie, A. (1975) Communication problems in Health
    Education in The Consumer Society, Journ. Royal
    Society Health, 3
Mateef, D. (1960) Morphological and Physiological
    Factors of Ageing, in Larson, L. Health and
    Fitness in a Modern World, American College
    of Sports & Medicine: Illinois
Matthews, D. (1973) Tests and Measurement in Physical
    Education, Saunders: Philadelphia
McEwen, J. Martini, C. and Wilkins, N. (1983) Partic-
    ipation in Health, Croom Helm: London
McKeown, K. (1976) The Role of Medicine, Nuffield
    Prov. Hos. Trust: London
Miller, H.C. (1963) The Aged Countryman, Nat. Corp.
    Care of Old People: London
Moore Smith, B. (1977) in Pearlman, C. (1977) Is
    geriatric medicine part of a G.P.'s training,
    Mod. Geriatrics, 2
Moss, M. (1979) Meaningfulness of time use by the
    elderly, Paper presented at Symposium of Leisure
    Research, National Recreation and Parks Assoc.
    Congress: New Orleans, Oct.
Musgrove, P. (1968) Curriculum Objectives, Journ.
    Curriculum Studies 1:1:5-1
Nat. Corp. Care of Old People (1973) Old Age - A
    register of Social Research, 1964-72, N.C.C.O.P.:

London
Nat. Assoc. Human Development (1976) Programmes
for Old Persons, N.A.H.D.: Washington
Nat. Assoc. Human Development, (1976) Join the Active
People over 60, N.A.H.D.: Washington
Nat. Assoc. Human Development, (1976) Exercise,
Diet and Nutrition for People over 60, N.A.H.D.:
Washington
Nat. Assoc. Human Development (1976) Basic Exercises
for people over 60, N.A.H.D.: Washington
Nat. Assoc. Human Development (1976) Moderate Exercises
for people over 60, N.A.H.D.: Washington
Nat. Assoc. Human Development (1976) Exercise - Activity
for people over 60, N.A.H.D.: Washington
Nat. Council on Aging (1974) Myth and Reality of
Ageing, I.C.P.S.R.: Michigan
Nat. Development Service, (1975) Communicating with
Pictures, U.N.I.C.E.F.
Nat. Therapeutic Rec. Service (1978) Approved Content
areas for 4 year Undergraduate Curricula, N.T.R.S.:
Washington
Nie et.al. (1970) Statistical Package for the Social
Services, McGraw Hill: N.Y.
Northedge, A. (1975) Learning through discussion,
Teaching at a distance, 2
Nottingham Univ. (1978) Health Questionnaire, unpub-
lished paper, Department of Community Medicine
O'Connell, P. (1978) Health Visitors Education at
University, Whitefriars: R.C.N.
Open University (1974) First Years of Life, Open
University
Open University (1978) Ageing in Society Units 1-4,
Open University
Open University (1978) Ageing in Society Units 5-8,
Open University
Open University, Health Education Council and Scot.
Health Ed. Dept. (1980) The Good Health Guide,
Harper & Row: London
Oppenheim, A. (1966) Questionnaire Design and Attitude
Measurement, Heinemann: London
Passmore, J. (1945) Talking Things Over, Melbourne
Univ.: Australia
Paterson, C.A. and Connolly, M. (1978) Therapeutic
Recreation Professional Preparation programmes
A State of the Art, Illinois University
Pearlman, C. (1977) Is geriatric medicine part of
a GPs Training Mod. Geriatrics, 2
Powell, C. and Crombie, A. (1974) The Kilsyth Question-
naire, Age and Ageing, 3
Presidental Sports Award, (1976) An Introduction
to Physical Fitness, H.E.W.: Washington

President's Council on Fitness and Sport (1978)
    National Adult Fitness, H.E.W.: Washington
Puner, M. (1974) To the Good Long Life, Open University
Rainsburg, J. (1954) There's life in the old dog
    yet, Rubery Owen
Raab (1961) Degenerative Heart Disease from lack
    of exercise, in Staley, S. (1961) Exercise
    and Fitness, University P.E. Dept. Athletic
    Institute: Illinois
Rapparport, R. and Rapparport, R.N. (1975) Leisure
    and the family cycle, R.K.P.: London
Reid, D. and Greene, W. (1971) Health and Modern
    Man, Macmillan: N.Y.
Rainbault, G. et.al. (1975) Aspects of communication
    between patient and doctors, Paediatrics, 55:3
Richardson, I. (1964) Age and Need, Livingstone:
    Edinburgh
Robins, J. (1978) Where to go to live longer, Woman's
    Own
Robinson, J.R. (1977) How Americans Use Time, Praeger:
    N.Y.
Rose, A. and Peterson, W. (1965) Older People and
    their Social World, Davis: Philadelphia
Rosen, G. (1960) Health Programmes for an Ageing
    Population in Tibbetts, C. (1960) Handbook
    of Social Gerontology: Chicago
Roscow, I. and Breslau, N. (1966) A Guttman Health
    Scale for the Aged, Journ. Geront. 24:1
Rothenberg, R. (1964) Health in Later Years, New
    American Library: N.Y.
Royal College of Nursing (1975), Improving Geriatric
    Care, R.C.N.: London
Rudd, T. (1967) Human Relationships in Old Age,
    Faber: London
Rudd, T. (1966) The Basis of Physical Health in
    Retirement, Geront, Clinica, 8:189:196
Russell, G. (1972) Teaching in Further Education,
    Pitman: London
Saunders, C.M. (1970) Training for the Practice
    of Clinical Gerontology - The Role of Social
    Medicine in Gitman, L. and Woodford Williams,
    E. (1970) Research, Training and Practice in
    Clinical Medicine of Ageing, Kaeger: Basle
Shoenrich, E.H. (1970) Some observations on the
    Requirements of Training Programmes in Geriatrics,
    in Gitman, L and Woodford Williams, E. (1970)
    Research, Training and Practice in Clinical
    Medicine of Ageing, Kaeger: Basle
Scot. Health Dept. (1977) Fit for Life, S.H.E.D.:
    Edinburgh
Suffolk Old Peopls Welfare Assoc. (1978) Newsletter,

S.O.P.W.A.
Seebohm et.al. (1968) Report of the Committee on
    L.A. and Allied Personal Social Services, (Seebohm
    Report), H.M.S.O.: London
Select Committee of the House of Lords, (1974) Sport
    and Leisure, H.M.S.O.: London
Shanas, E. (1962) The Health of Older People, Harvard
    University: Mass.
Shanas, E. et.al. (1968) Old People in Three Industrial
    Societies, R.K.P.: London
Sheldon, J. (1958) Society and its Older Members,
    Journ. Royal Society of Health, 4
Shenfield B.P. and Allen, I. (1972) Organisation
    and Voluntary Services, P.E.P.: London
Shephard, R. (1969) Endurance Fitness, University
    Toronto
Shephard, R. (1978) Physical Activity and Aging,
    Croom Helm: London
Shore, E. (1970) Career Choices in Medicine, Health
    Trends, 2:3
Sidney, K. and Shephard, R. (1977) Activity Patterns
    of elderly men and women, Journ. Geront. 32:25-32
Slusher, H. and Lockhart, A. (1966) Anthology of
    contemporary readings - An Introduction to
    Physical Education, Brown: Iowa
Smith, H. (1968) Introduction to Human Movement,
    Addison-Wellsley: Mass
Snellgrove, D. (1963) Elderly Housebound, White
    Crescent: London
Sports Council (1978) Trim Trails, Sports Council:
    London
Sports Council (South Region) (1978) Sport for the
    Not So Young Report, Sports Council (Southern
    Report): Reading
Stacey, M. (1976) Health and Health Policy, S.S.R.C.:
    London
Staley, S. (1960) Exercise and Fitness, Amer. Coll.
    Sports. Med.: Illinois
Stein and Sessions (1977) Recreation and Special
    Age Groups, Holbrook: Boston
Stephenson, D. (1968) Specialisation within a Unified
    Social Work Service, Case Conference, 15:5,
    184-189
Storrs, A. (1976) Geriatric Nursing. Balliere Tindall
Swardlaw, A. et.al. (1979) Career Preferences of
    Pre-Registration House Offices in Oxford Region
    and Secular Trends in Career Choice, Health
    Trends, 11
Szalai, A. (ed) (1972) The Use of Time, Mouton:
    Holland
Taba, H. (1971) The functions of a conceptual framework

for curriculum design in Hooper, R. (1971)
Curriculum: Context and Development, Oliver
and Boyd: London
Taylor, P. (1971) Purpose and structure in the curr-
iculum in Hooper, R. (1971) Curriculum: Context
and Development, Oliver and Boyd: London
Thorton, E.B. (1967) A Community Health Team, Journal
Royal Society of Health, 4
Tibbitts, C. (1960) Handbook of Social Gerontology:
Chicago
Tinkler, A. (1981) The Elderly in Modern Society,
Longman: London
Tones, B.K. (1977) Effectiveness and Efficiency
in Health Education, Scot. Health Ed. Dept.:
Edinburgh
Townsend, P. (1970) The Fifth Social Service - A
Criticial Analysis of the Seebohm Report, Fabian:
London
Townsend, P. (1970) The objectives of the New Local
Social Services, Fabian: London
Townsend, P. and Wedderburn, D. (1965) The Aged
in the Welfare State, Bell: London
Tunbridge, R. (1971) Rehabilitation, D.H.S.S.:
London
Tunstall, J. (1967) Old and Alone, R.K.P.: London
van Meirhaegue (1972) Health and Social Services
for the Ageing, Journ. Royal Society of Health: 4
Vedder, G. (1963) Gerontology - A Book of Readings,
Thomas: Illlinois
Ward, R. (1979) The Ageing Experience, Lippencott:
Philadelphia
Warren, M. (1960) The Evolution of Geriatric Medicine,
Geront. Clinica, 2:17
Wedgewood, J. (1972) The Future of Geriatrics, Age
and Ageing, 1:2
Weston, T. and Ashworth, R. (1963) Old People in
Britain, Bow: London
Williams, J.G.P. (1965) Medical Aspects of Sport
and Physical Fitness, Pergamon: London
Williams, J.G.P. and Sperryn, P. (1976) Sports Medicine,
Edward Arnold: London
Wilson, M. (1975) Health is for People, Darton,
Longman, Todd: London
Winchester, J. (1965) Blood Pressure - What's New?
Readers Digest, 10
Woolf, J. (1961) Prevention of Disease through Exercise
and Health Education, in Larsen, L. (1961)
Health in a Modern World, Amer. Coll. of Sport
and Med.: Illinois
World Health Organization (1978) Habitual Physical
Activity and Health, W.H.O.

World Health Organization (1974) <u>Planning and Organ-</u>
<u>isation of Geriatric Services</u>, W.H.O.
Wright, I.J. (1976) <u>British Social Services</u>, Macdonald
Evans: London
Wright, W.B. (1972) Geriatrics and General Medicine,
<u>Age and Ageing</u>, 1:20
Yarvote et.al. (1974) Organisation and Evaluation
of Physical Fitness Programmes in Industry,
<u>Journ. Occup. Med.</u> 16:9, 589-598
Younghusband E. (1977) Is Old Age a Good Age? <u>Community</u>
<u>Care</u> 7:12
Zaborowski, M. (1962) Ageing and Recreation, <u>Journal</u>
<u>Geront.</u> 17:302-309

Appendix A

LEISURETIME ACTIVITY PARTICIPATION BY PROFESSION

The table details are taken from the Macheath (1982) study illustrating the differences in participation levels between the various professions that work with the elderly in a variety of situations.

SRN/SEN/Nurse Aide by Regular Leisuretime Activities Participation

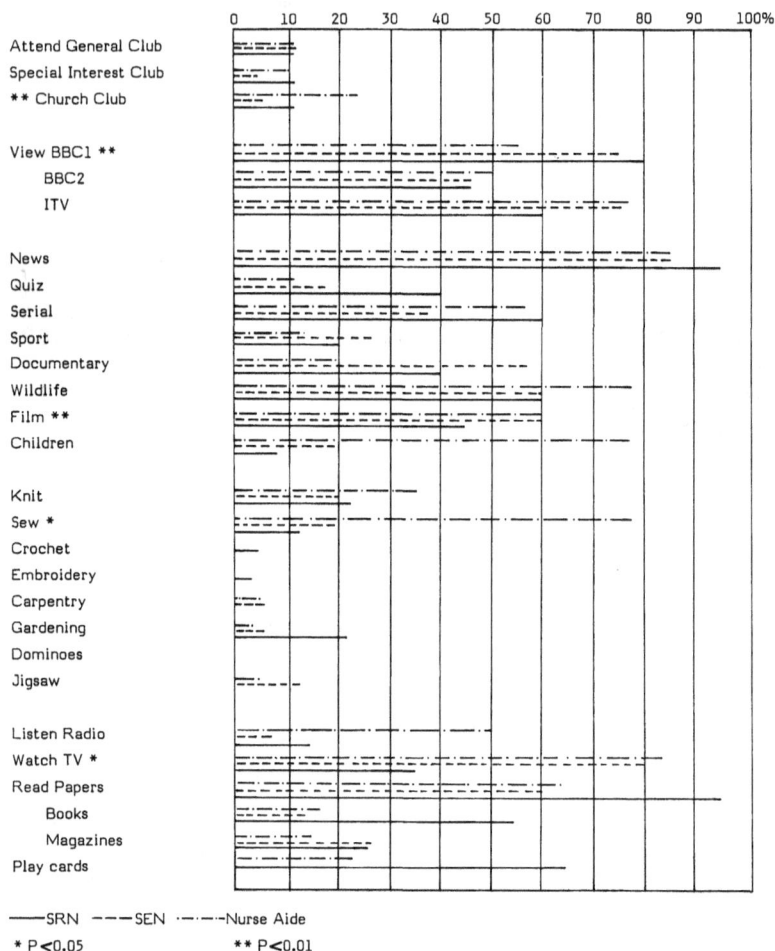

| | 0 | 10 | 20 | 30 | 40 | 50 | 60 | 70 | 80 | 90 | 100% |

Attend General Club
Special Interest Club
** Church Club

View BBC1 **
BBC2
ITV

News
Quiz
Serial
Sport
Documentary
Wildlife
Film **
Children

Knit
Sew *
Crochet
Embroidery
Carpentry
Gardening
Dominoes
Jigsaw

Listen Radio
Watch TV *
Read Papers
Books
Magazines
Play cards

———SRN   － － －SEN   ·—·—·Nurse Aide
* P<0.05   ** P<0.01

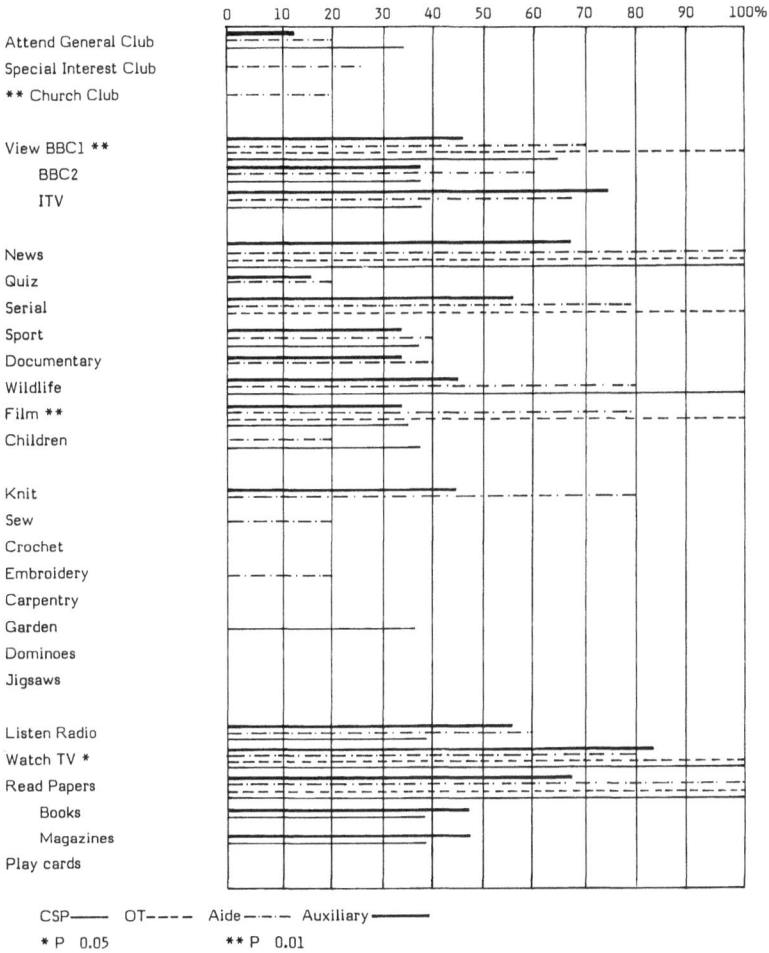

CSP/OT/CSP OT Aide by Regular Leisuretime Activities Participation

CSP——— OT－－－ Aide —·—· Auxiliary ———
* P 0.05   ** P 0.01

P.E./P.E. (Nil)/Age Concern (Nil) Elderly (Nil) by Leisuretime Activities Participation

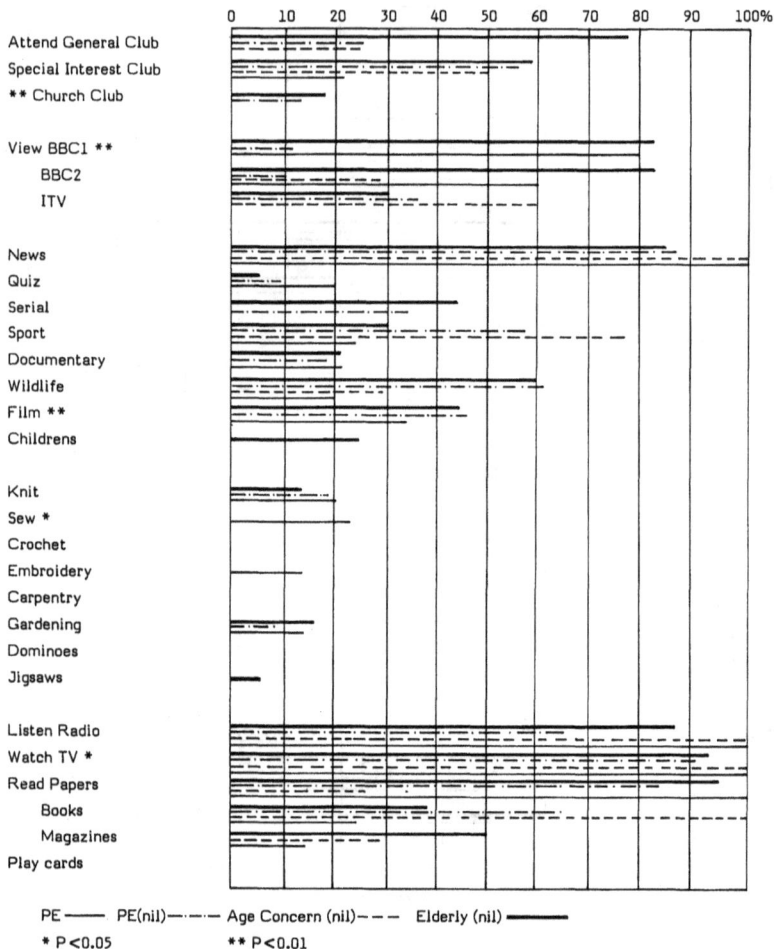

```
                    0    10   20   30   40   50   60   70   80   90  100%
Attend General Club
Special Interest Club
** Church Club

View BBC1 **
      BBC2
      ITV

News
Quiz
Serial
Sport
Documentary
Wildlife
Film **
Childrens

Knit
Sew *
Crochet
Embroidery
Carpentry
Gardening
Dominoes
Jigsaws

Listen Radio
Watch TV *
Read Papers
      Books
      Magazines
Play cards
```

PE ——— PE(nil)—·—·— Age Concern (nil)— — — Elderly (nil) ———
* P<0.05   ** P<0.01

Appendix B

UNDERSTANDING OF ELDERLY PARTICIPATION IN SELECTED ACTIVITIES BY PROFESSION

The table details are taken from the Macheath (1982) study illustrating the differences in the understanding of elderly participation levels between the various professions that work with the elderly in a variety of situations.

SRN/SEN/Nurse Aide by Understanding of Regular Activity Patterns in Old Age

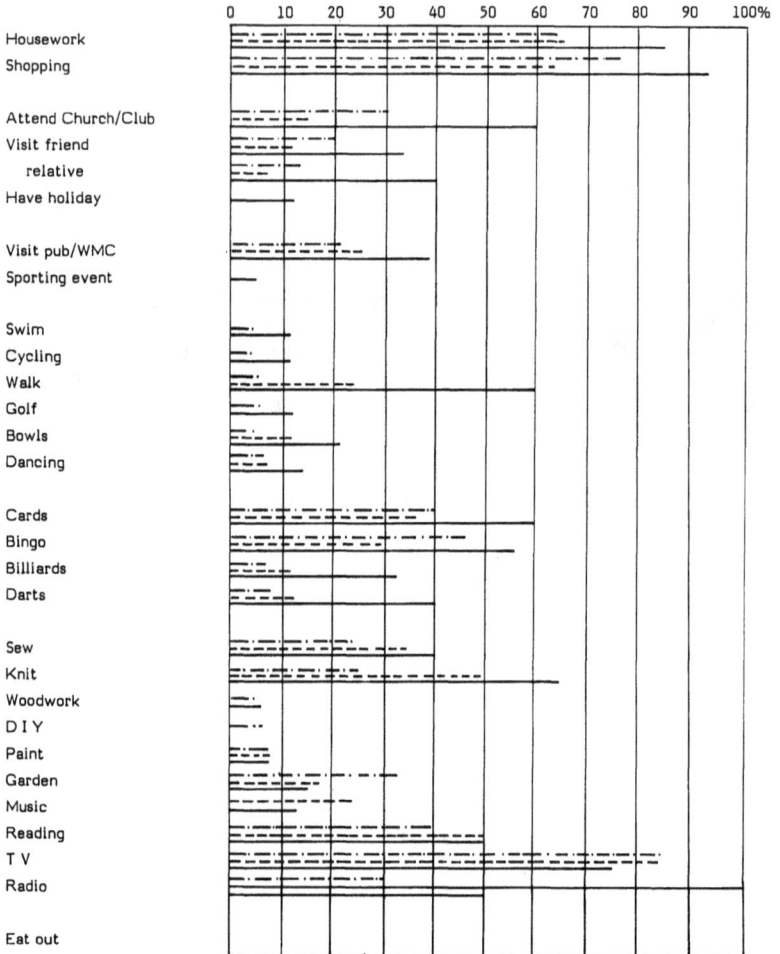

Housework
Shopping

Attend Church/Club
Visit friend
  relative
Have holiday

Visit pub/WMC
Sporting event

Swim
Cycling
Walk
Golf
Bowls
Dancing

Cards
Bingo
Billiards
Darts

Sew
Knit
Woodwork
DIY
Paint
Garden
Music
Reading
TV
Radio

Eat out

SRN ——— SEN ——— Nurse Aide —·—·—
* P<0.05   ** P<0.01

CSP/OT/CO Aide/Auxiliary by Understanding of Regular Physical Activity in Old Age

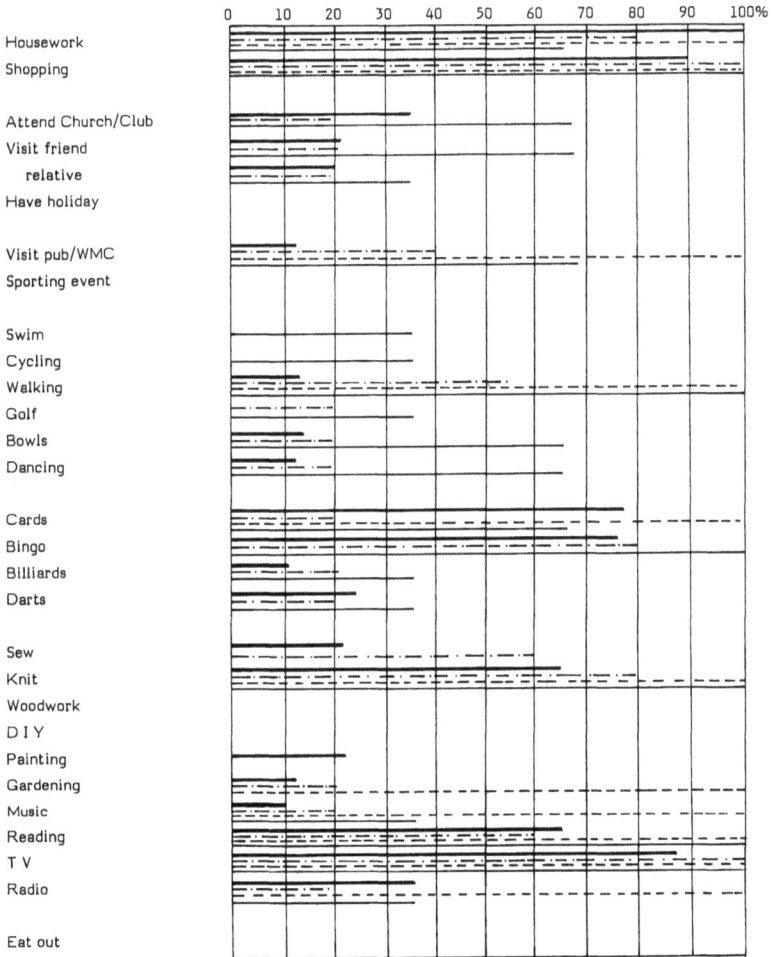

CSP ——— OT ---- Aide —··— Auxiliary ━━━

* P<0.05   ** P<0.01

159

P.E./P.E. (Nil)/Age Concern (Nil) Elderly (Nil) by Understanding of Regular Activity Patterns in Old Age

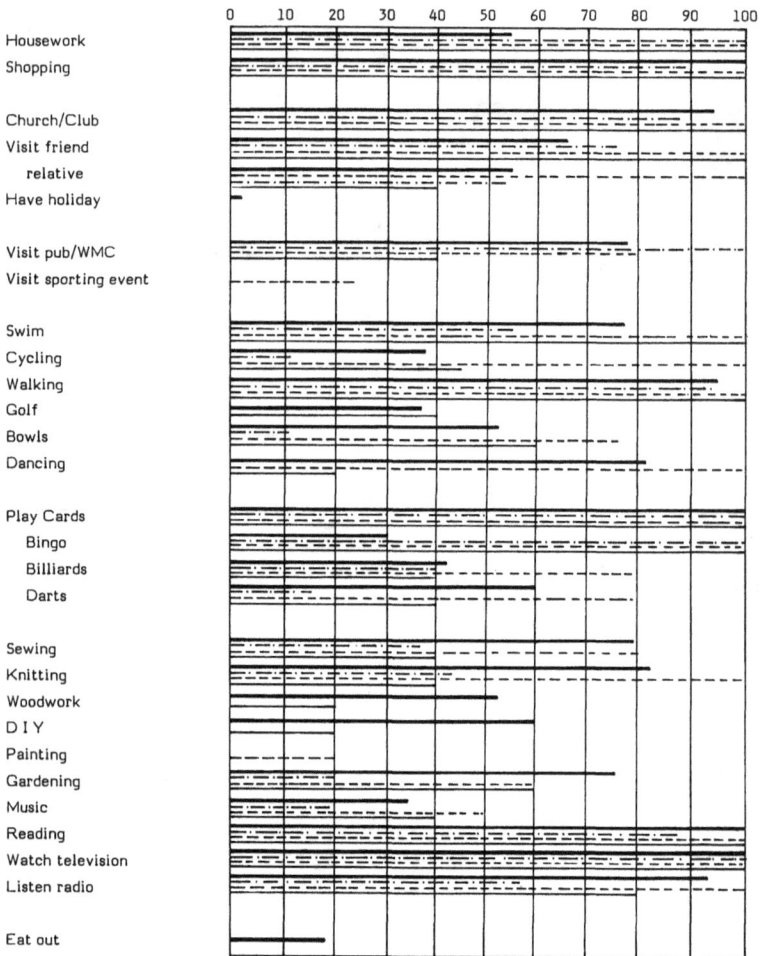

```
                    0   10  20  30  40  50  60  70  80  90  100

Housework
Shopping

Church/Club
Visit friend
  relative
Have holiday

Visit pub/WMC
Visit sporting event

Swim
Cycling
Walking
Golf
Bowls
Dancing

Play Cards
  Bingo
  Billiards
  Darts

Sewing
Knitting
Woodwork
D I Y
Painting
Gardening
Music
Reading
Watch television
Listen radio

Eat out
```

P.E.——P.E. (Nil)———— Age Concern (Nil)—·—··Elderly (Nil)——

	U29	30-34	35-39	40-44	45-49	50-54	55-59	60-64	65-69	70-74	75-79	80+
Regularly Attend Club												
General	12	0	30	6	8	8	33	60	73	83	90	45
Special Interest	8	30	0	18	16	16	18	0	83	75	70	40
Church	20	0	8	6	10	0	8	0	55	45	45	40
Regularly View BBC1	45	60	75	75	65	80	70	90	75	83	75	65
BBC2	25	0	25	33	8	45	55	50	42	42	33	30
ITV	55	80	65	78	40	33	33	33	4	8	0	8
Listen to Radio Daily	72	68	52	62	8	70	72	78	93	93	90	85
occasionally	22	8	28	30	18	3	25	22	2	0	0	14
Watch Television Daily	60	100	90	93	93	95	95	75	70	78	68	65
occasionally	8	0	8	4	5	4	0	22	4	4	0	12
View Regularly News	90	100	100	100	100	90	90	85	70	70	73	73
quiz	50	30	28	55	33	55	54	55	60	68	68	48
serial	85	90	90	82	75	90	90	85	55	83	65	58
film	85	100	90	82	50	64	70	83	60	72	78	55
documentary	65	83	70	95	83	100	90	100	70	80	75	75
wildlife	75	88	93	90	100	100	94	100	70	78	75	66
sport	55	75	60	55	33	78	72	72	54	55	44	50
childrens programmes	43	55	30	45	22	38	38	52	60	64	60	64

Activity												
Swim Regularly	16	45	55	75	50	18	0	0	12	12	22	15
occasionally	0	4	8	16	12	18	8	24	25	28	30	44
Walk Regularly	54	90	92	100	88	46	72	42	64	36	38	54
occasionally	12	8	0	0	16	56	18	58	20	44	62	44
Knit Regularly	25	28	33	50	72	55	44	50	42	40	8	20
occasionally	25	28	34	16	0	28	33	16	12	33	33	0
Sew regularly	24	34	22	28	36	36	36	33	28	18	0	12
occasionally	44	44	36	33	26	44	28	34	28	40	45	33
Embroider occasionally	15	25	30	46	12	18	10	18	18	4	6	15
Crochet occasionally	55	60	50	58	10	18	0	0	6	0	8	18
Garden occasionally	20	54	33	58	60	82	60	40	82	33	52	33
Carpentry occasionally	8	20	30	28	25	10	0	8	10	4	10	8
Dominoes occasionally	20	25	25	25	0	15	0	0	10	8	0	8
Jigsaws occasionally	42	72	75	80	22	25	28	18	50	28	18	25
Reads papers daily	80	100	96	100	100	82	72	66	82	76	76	54
books daily	50	52	48	58	38	28	33	15	30	20	28	24
magazines daily	12	4	8	0	12	0	28	0	30	20	30	12

Appendix D % BY AGE AND UNDERSTANDING OF ELDERLY PARTICIPATION IN SELECTED ACTIVITIES REGULARLY

	U29	30-34	35-39	40-44	45-49	50-54	55-59	60-64	65-69	70-74	75-79	80+
Housework daily	33	22	22	50	15	26	55	64	95	95	93	70
1/week	33	70	22	38	50	54	16	36	4	4	4	30
Shop food daily	30	15	22	42	24	55	25	62	100	100	100	84
1/week	46	72	58	42	58	44	55	28	0	0	0	18
Occasional Holiday	52	20	30	50	8	20	72	88	100	100	94	90
Pub/WMC Regularly	36	24	30	20	18	42	55	78	78	90	80	72
occasionally	40	45	42	55	78	42	28	22	22	4	15	28
Sports Events Regularly	4	0	0	0	0	0	0	0	0	0	0	8
occasionally	45	30	32	40	46	50	45	62	83	85	72	72
Swim Regularly	12	8	12	18	40	6	15	50	78	80	66	33
occasionally	12	25	2	2	25	12	0	0	15	12	20	25
Walk Regularly	30	15	20	40	38	40	58	80	75	93	100	93
occasionally	40	75	50	30	38	52	15	12	4	0	0	4
Golf Occasionally	28	12	10	18	15	10	28	50	100	80	100	80
Cycle Occasionally	30	12	12	25	8	10	36	50	100	94	84	48
Bowls Occasionally	42	54	42	64	30	80	72	100	100	100	100	97
Dance Occasionally	48	50	25	75	50	36	44	60	100	97	94	90

Cards Regularly	55	48	38	60	50	96	72	83	94	100	100	97
Bingo Regularly	55	40	55	50	50	66	76	72	33	44	60	66
Billiards Regularly	25	8	4	15	15	18	18	25	38	60	35	45
Darts Regularly	25	6	15	25	28	30	33	28	70	100	55	75
Knit Regularly	52	24	64	50	50	65	52	100	95	97	90	92
Sew Regularly	33	15	18	33	33	36	45	62	97	95	85	75
Woodwork Occasionally	42	25	18	33	25	36	18	50	58	95	92	92
D I Y Occasionally	33	25	18	33	32	18	18	64	95	97	90	85
Decorating Occasionally	42	25	28	36	33	18	26	28	64	88	90	64
Garden Occasionally	48	46	32	62	58	65	65	62	100	97	97	95
Music Regularly	26	22	0	20	8	45	18	25	78	72	72	64
Read Regularly	75	58	30	52	68	40	72	72	65	95	100	90
Television Regularly	92	70	95	78	92	100	100	88	95	90	95	90
Radio Regularly	55	58	40	45	33	44	65	88	100	100	97	92
Eat Out Occasionally	38	15	32	45	50	33	33	50	95	100	92	92

Appendix E

THE MACHEATH (1982) STUDY

THE GENERAL APPROACH

The responses were collected by means of a questionnaire and structured interview. Once the data had been collated and classified it was possible to consider the relationship of the responses to one another and their broader significance. The responses were scanned for associations between the variables. Sections A-E were completed on the IBM 6600 using the S.P.S.S. (1970). Relevant cross tabulations were investigated; significance considered and the frequencies of responses within the two populations (staff and elderly) compared.

The study sought to obtain data to illustrate to what degree those who work with the elderly appreciate and understand the types of activity engaged in by their elderly patients and how these same elderly patients view health and fitness in relation to their daily living and independence in the community. This involved exploring the physical activities participated in by the elderly and the staff who work with them; the understanding of the elderly and the staff of the physical activity participation of the elderly generally; and how both the staff and their elderly patients envisaged health and good physical condition.

This study is in no way exhaustive but it was felt it would answer some of the pertinent questions of immediate relevance to the problems of rehabilitation of the elderly and the training of staff in the rehabilitative field who advise the elderly regarding mobility and fitness relative to their independence in the community and daily living activities.

The descriptive study undertaken endeavoured to obtain specific information from two groups of individuals making up the target population: (a) the elderly (b) staff in a variety of Health, Education and Social Services professions who work with them.

DATA COLLECTION

The universal baseline data was collected by means of a checklist questionnaire completed by the interviewer. An ordinal scale was used. The aspects of activity were investigated through the closed question techniques as there was a known range of possible responses which could accurately describe the participation of all respondents. By the use of the closed question more questions could be asked and responded to in a given time which was particularly important when interviewing the elderly. It was felt that the spontaniety of open questions was not necessary in this instance. The wording of the closed question was aimed at communicating with respondents of all ages and backgrounds. Sentences were kept short and language simple with each question expressing one idea.

The activity list was developed as a result of a literature search. Studies were scanned for physical activities, leisure pursuits, hobbies and pastimes. Respondents were asked to indicate how often they participated in these activities on a five point scale - daily to never. A similar procedure was adopted in the development of the lists of activities the target population believed elderly people participated in. These were grouped to facilitate ease of presentation and response.

Resulting from the pilot study (Macheath 1978) it was found necessary for all the questionnaires to be adminstered by the researcher rather than being self administered. Many of the elderly in the pilot study had failing eyesight and/or poor pencil control whilst several of the trial group had reading and/or comprehension problems. This aspect of the questionnaire thus became an administered, structured one.

It was decided that despite the increased time involved the researcher would conduct all the standardized questionnaire interviews. Interviewer variation cannot be totally controlled even if the same interviewer is used as she may unwittingly vary the approach with different respondents. However many problems related to interviewer bias can be reduced through the use of a simple interviewer following a sound pilot study and pretest experience

166

when unforseen difficulties can be resolved.

THE SAMPLE POPULATION

The sample populations were staff and elderly who
live and/or work in one District Health Authority in
South East England. Each group consisted of 150
individuals. It was not possible to balance the ratio
of men and women in either of the groups as the
individuals available in each instance at the time of
the arranged initial visit were interviewed. It must
be remembered that had this initial visit been the
previous day or the following day to the arranged
one, the structure of the groups may have been very
different. This will need bearing in mind when the
results are considered.

Only one member of the hospital staff was in the
60-64 years age group, all the others were below the
age of sixty years. Twenty two of the staff were
elderly themselves working at the Clubs for the
elderly used in the study. The majority of elderly
were aged over seventy years with 35.3% of them being
over eighty years, thus the data is weighted towards
the older elderly rather than the recently retired.

By interviewing the staff and elderly available
at the time of the initial visit the balancing of
numbers in the respective age groups was precluded.
However, there appears to be sufficient in each age
group, except 60-64 years, to make balanced
considerations between the various groups. It was not
possible to balance either between the staff and the
elderly in the different Institutions visited. Night
staff were interviewed in two hospitals where their
daytime peers had been interviewed. However the
elderly were not interviewed at this time (after
midnight) but were interviewed at the same time as
the daytime staff in these Institutions.

Approximately 66.0% of the staff and 33.0% of
the elderly are to be found in the five small
geriatric units and are general hospital ward
utilised in the study. The rest of the staff sample
are involved either individually or as salaried Club
staff, or as voluntary Club Staff in the few Clubs
used for the investigations - one Lunch Club for the
Elderly; one Tea Centre/Social Centre for the Elderly
close to the High Street; one Club for Disabled
Elderly; and one large Club for the Elderly basically
serving those who had moved at various times from the
East End of London. The elderly members using these
Clubs account for 66.0% approximatley of the elderly

population, living independent lives to varying degrees in the community. The hospital elderly include acute bed and long stay bed individuals.

THE QUESTIONNAIRE

Concepts of Fitness in the Elderly

Please indicate your age group

(A) Under 29 years   1   55-59 years   7

Under 29 years	1	55-59 years	7
30-34 years	2	60-64 years	8
35-39 years	3	65-69 years	9
40-44 years	4	70-74 years	10
45-49 years	5	75-79 years	11
50-54 years	6	Over 80 years	12

PLEASE COMPLETE THE FOLLOWING BACKGROUND DETAILS
BY CHECKING THE APPROPRIATE BOX

Male	1
Female	2

Do you live in:

House	1
Bungalow	2
Flat	3
Bedsit	4
Hospital	5
Home	6
Other (specify)	7

Do you live on:

Own	1
With spouse	2
With friend	3
With relations	4
Other	5

(B) Do you attend:

	Regularly	Occasionally	Never
General interest club			
Special interest club			
Church club			
Other (specify)			

169

Which televison stations do you watch

	Regularly	Occasionally	Never
BBC1			
BBC2			
ITV			

Which types of programmes do you watch:

	Regularly	Occasionally	Never
News			
Quizzes			
Serials			
Sport			
Documentaries			
Wildlife			
Films			
Childrens			
Other (Specify)			

(C) <u>How often do you take part in these activities?</u>

	Every day	Once week	Once month	Occasionally	Never
Swimming					
Walking					
Bowls					
Dancing					
Darts					
Snooker					
Chess					
Fishing					
Knitting					
Sewing					
Crochet					
Embroidery					
Gardening					
Dominoes					
Jigsaws					
Listen radio					
Watch TV					
Read papers					
Read books					
Read magazines					
Play cards					

ELDERLY ONLY

(D) Do you do the following activities with:

	no help	stick	crutches	zimmer	with help	wheel-chair	not able to
walk outside							
walk inside							
go to shops							
walk from shops							
walk upstairs							
walk down-stairs							
get into bed							
get out of bed							
get into chair							
get out of chair							
prepare a meal							
do house-hold chores							

(E) How many years experience have you had in:

Hospitals   Community nursing

Day hospitals   Current situation

Day centres

What contact do you have with the elderly? Is it:

in hospital	1	individually	1
at hospital day centre	2	in groups	2
residential home	3	at clubs	3
in their home	4	others (specify)	4
at a clinic	5		
in your office	6		
at information centre	7		

Please list your professional qualification, including post basic special qualifications

SRN	1	Night Auxiliary	8
SEN	2	P.E.	9
Nurse Aide	3	P.E. student (nil)	10
CSP	4	Age Concern (nil)	11
CT	5	Elderly (nil)	12
CSP/OT Aide	6	Other	13
Auxiliary	7		

PART II

(F) Please indicate how regularly you think elderly people in general take part in the following activities by placing an 'X' in the appropriate column

	Every day	Frequently i.e.1/2 per week	Regularly each month	Occasion- ally	Never
Housework with no outside help					
Shopping for food					
Attend a meeting at a Church/Club etc					
Visit a friend					
Visit a relative					
Have a holiday					
Visit the Pub/Mens Club					
Go to a Sporting Event					
Participate in: Swimming Cycling Walking Golf Bowls Dancing					
Play cards bingo billiards darts					
Participate in a hobby sewing knitting woodwork D I Y painting gardening music reading television radio					
Eat out somewhere					

174

(G) Please complete the following sentences in any way you think fit:

1. Exercise is

2. When I think of exercise I

3. Talking to other about exercise is

4. Elderly who exercise

5. If I could exercise I

6. My worst fears about exercise are

7. Activity is only enjoyable if

(H) Exercise for the Over 60s

In the spaces below please indicate the main and minor points that struck you as you saw the slides

Main Points   Minor Points   Other Details

INDEX

177

178

For Product Safety Concerns and Information please contact our EU
representative GPSR@taylorandfrancis.com
Taylor & Francis Verlag GmbH, Kaufingerstraße 24, 80331 München, Germany